WINNING TENNIS THROUGH MENTAL TOUGHNESS

WINNING TENNIS THROUGH MENTAL TOUGHNESS

by Walter A. Luszki, Ed. D.

PREFACE BY J. DONALD BUDGE

NEW YORK EVEREST HOUSE PUBLISHERS

Acknowledgments & Dedication

Special appreciation goes to Sol Marshall, President, Creative Book Company, who authorized the use of any appropriate material from my *Psych Yourself to Better Tennis*, now published by Melvin Powers of Wilshire Book Company.

Thanks to James Beck, executive sports editor, *Post-Courier*, Charleston, South Carolina, for many of the photographs appearing in this book. Thanks also to Russ Adams, contributing photographer for *World Tennis* and *Tennis USA*, and to Roy Barth, tennis pro at Kiawah Island, South Carolina, for other photographs in the book. Information in some of the chapters has appeared in articles in *World Tennis* and *Tennis USA*, the publishers and editors of which have given permission to use them in this book.

In some instances it has been necessary to disguise the identities of top-ranking players and associates described, but the descriptions and the incidents cited are accurate.

I wish to thank all the players who have helped me learn about the psychology of tennis. My hundreds of opponents, both winners and losers, in some 300 tournaments in which I have participated, have contributed to my understanding of psychology in tennis, and enriched my enjoyment of the game.

Finally, I thank my wife, Margaret, a Ph.D. in psychology from the University of Michigan. Her encouragement and support made this book possible.

—Walter A. Luszki

Library of Congress Cataloging in Publication Data:

Luszki, Walter A.
   Winning tennis through mental toughness.

   1. Tennis — Psychological aspects.   I. Title.
GV1002.9.P75L87   796.342'01   81-19537
ISBN: 0-89696-150-8   AACR2

Copyright © 1982 by Walter A. Luszki, Ed.D.
All Rights Reserved
Published in 1982 by Everest House, Publishers
33 West 60th Street, New York, N.Y. 10023
Published simultaneously in Canada by
Beaverbooks, Don Mills, Ontario
Manufactured in the United States of America
First Edition   HL282

Contents

	Preface by J. Donald Budge	6
1	Mental Toughness — The Key to Winning Tennis	7
2	How to Develop Determination	13
3	How to Improve Concentration	25
4	Anxiety and the Would-Be Winner	40
5	Twenty-four Ways to Control Anxiety and Thus Boost Confidence	47
6	Psychological Preparation for Tournament Tennis	57
7	On Capturing Momentum in a Match	66
8	Know Your Opponent and Playing Conditions	71
9	Psychological Warfare	79
	Epilogue	93

Preface

Dr. Luszki's *Winning Tennis through Mental Toughness* is an important contribution to the psychology of tennis. Tennis players generally agree that there are three basic areas that require development if one is to become a champion.

The first is stroking ability. This is the mechanics of the game, such as how to develop the forehand, backhand, smash, and other strokes. Excellent strokes alone, however, are generally not sufficient to carry one to the semi-finals.

Next is physical conditioning. The player who is in the best physical condition does not always win the tournament, but the person in poor physical condition is most unlikely to win, despite other assets.

Third is mental toughness and training. The top 200 world-ranked players have about equal stroking ability and are generally in excellent physical shape, but there are big differences in their degrees of mental toughness. Mental toughness, as Dr. Luszki points out, basically includes three characteristics: *determination, concentration, confidence*.

The aim of Dr. Luszki's book is to help develop these three crucial characteristics. The book contains step-by-step information to help a player attain better determination, concentration, and confidence and to develop the right psychological frame of mind and personality to win. The book offers other tips to help win in tennis. These include suggestions and ideas on psychological preparation for tournament play, how to capture momentum in tennis, the importance of knowing your opponent's strengths and weaknesses, gamesmanship and psychological warfare, and how to use behavior modification to improve your game.

I recommend Dr. Luszki's *Winning Tennis through Mental Toughness* to you since it will help you develop an important part of tennis training, namely, mental toughness.

—J. Donald Budge

Chapter 1

Mental Toughness— The Key to Winning Tennis

Napoleon is reported once to have remarked, "The mental is to the physical as a hundred is to one." He was speaking of war, but anyone who thinks about his own successes and failures, or those of others, will come to see that the mental is to the physical as a hundred is to one in most areas of life. Think of such ordinary activities as driving an automobile and dancing. We tend to think of these as primarily physical activities, since we see physical motion. But if we reflect on them we observe that the success with which we perform them is largely a matter of our mental state. The driver who keeps his eye on the road and his mind on what he is doing drives safely. The driver who doesn't risks disaster. If you've ever admired the ease and grace of a couple on a dance floor, what you were admiring was the result of confidence based on knowledge and ability, which were acquired through determination and concentration.

What is true of ordinary activities is true of extraordinary ones, especially those that, like tennis at its toughest, involve stress, exertion, endurance, and what Ernest Hemingway called "grace under pressure." It is not uncommon to hear a report of a physically frail woman lifting an overturned car or the huge trunk of a fallen tree to save her child from being crushed to death. Such an act is certainly physical. But if you consider that in ordinary circumstances the same woman might find it hard to raise a car with a jack and lift a spare tire into position, Napoleon's remark, quoted in the opening paragraph, seems no exaggeration.

The subject of this book may be thought of as the subject of Napoleon's remark: tennis is a kind of war. Everything that will be said here is in keeping with the great general's opinion about the relation between the mental and the physical. Tennis is, of course, a physical activity—as is war. Like war, tennis demands a combatant who keeps in good physical condition, who works to develop his abilities, and who values experience for what it can teach. This book will therefore instruct you in how to develop the mental side of your game in order to improve all of the key elements of winning tennis, including the physical and the technical.

You will come across many anecdotes—brief stories involving professionals who are well known, professionals who were once well known, and amateurs whose experiences are instructive to other amateurs. If you want to make real progress toward becoming the best player within your circle of fellow players, or at your club, it is not enough to read through good ideas and advice. You must absorb them so that they actually operate in you and do something for your game. The many anecdotes included here illustrate and support practical ideas and suggestions, implanting them firmly in the readers' minds. I hope that when you have finished the book and set it aside, the tips on developing your mental toughness will have become part of your tennis-playing personality.

Winning tennis at the higher levels of competition depends on four things: physical well-being, skill, experience, and mental toughness. When the best are competing, all four are working together. But it is mental toughness, or mental discipline, that makes it possible for such players to acquire the other three. Mental toughness means determination, concentration, and confidence. Of the three, determination is the most basic. It's most evident when a champion is in action—every effort of a Connors or an Evert Lloyd is directed to victory. What is not so evident is that such determination had to operate for a long time, day in and day out, before the champion could develop the physical capacity and the technical ability needed for victory.

The career of Billie Jean King provides a striking instance of how determination leads to getting into top shape and developing championship-level ability. Her success at Wimbledon was the result of her determined resolve not to give in to any desire other than the desire to be the champion, the best. Look into the careers of other top-notch players—of Jack Kramer, Rod Laver, Bjorn Borg—and you'll see the exact same kind of determination at work. Chris Evert, when once asked what she attributed her success to, gave an answer that amounts to a definition of determination in action: "Work, work, work."

To develop ability, to get into condition for tournament play, and to maintain a peak of ability and physical condition, it is necessary to overcome natural resistance to the sacrifices demanded. Determination does just this. What is often not realized is that well-developed abilities may be powerless against well-developed *habitual* abilities. When the ability to hit a tennis ball to wherever we want is a habit, our minds are free to attend to the other things that are happening the instant we hit it and to the things that will happen an instant later. When you can play with this kind of habitual skill, you will beat an opponent whose skills are equal to, or perhaps greater than yours, but not as habitual. Making a skill a habit requires as much determination as developing the skill in the first place.

If you have determination, you are likely to develop concentration, the second of the components of mental toughness. When Borg started to pursue his goal of winning all the major tournaments and becoming the best player in the world, poor concentration was his chief obstacle. One of the ways he improved his concentration was to go through each practice as if it were a match. As a result, he was able to display unshakable concentration, and also confidence, when he faced Adriano Panatta in Rome's notorious "Lion's Pit" for the 1978 Ital-

Bjorn Borg hits high-bouncing, heavy topspin shots. His coach, Lennart Bergelin, says that the Swedish wonder is one of the most iron-willed, persistent, and mentally tough players in the world. He has great endurance, strength, and a marvelous physique. The Golden King of the Courts has won five consecutive championships at Wimbledon (1976–80), five French Opens (1974, '75, and '78–80), three United States Pro titles (1974–76), and the World Championship of Tennis. He practices the way he plays: with intensity and determination.

ian Open Tennis Championship. In previous matches of that tournament, a boisterous and mercilessly partisan crowd of 10,000 had unnerved and demoralized Panatta's opponents, Vitas Gerulaitis, Hank Pfister, Victor Amaya, and Jose Higueras (Higueras walked off the court in the semifinal match against Panatta). During Borg's match, the crowd kept throwing coins until center court seemed a sort of Trevi Fountain. The Swede's self-possession nearly broke, but his ability to concentrate held fast, kept his game together, and led to his victory.

A lack of confidence, or a case of the jitters, may be more damaging to the would-be champion than weak strokes. Top-flight pros have lost big matches more often because of a defeatist attitude that suddenly overtook them or an inability to control anxiety than because of a lack of a particular skill. This book will have much to say about the ways to suppress anxiety and gain confidence. For now, it's enough to note a connection between determination and confidence: determination in the form of hard, long, and continual practice subjects a player to psychological as well as physical stress. Conditioning yourself to withstand such stress contributes greatly to the development of confidence.

Many of those reading this book may at this point object, "Sure, determination, concentration, and confidence are tremendously important, but if I wasn't born with the physical equipment of a Borg or an Evert how can I expect my game ever to compare with theirs?" From my observations of both men and women players, I can say that there is not much difference in physical capacity—or, for that matter, in stroke production—between players ranked among the ten best in the world and players ranked between the fortieth and the fiftieth best. What's more, there are tens of thousands of young men and women who equal or surpass Connors or Borg, Evert or Austin, in strength, agility, speed, lung capacity, and reactive quickness. My point is not that an invalid can win at Wimbledon but that the combination of physical attributes necessary to do so is no rarity. In a healthy young man or woman, a winning combination of mental characteristics should be the chief concern, and much can be done to develop these.

This is not just one man's opinion. Many of the best players have said as much. Kramer, Gonzales, Segura, and others have remarked that there are hundreds of players who are in excellent physical condition and have excellent strokes, mobility, and reflexes, but who lack the mental toughness to become outstanding. They may not be determined to improve their skills and make them habitual; they may not be able to concentrate sufficiently to keep off-the-court concerns from infringing on their play; or they may not have the confidence that dispels debilitating anxiety and tension.

Like physical condition, playing skill should be properly assessed in regard to its importance. Certainly, it is tremendously important—one of the four components of winning tennis. But the developing player should be aware that there have been many players with weaknesses or flaws in their strokes, yet who managed to defeat players with better strokes. Budge Patty was a Wimbledon champion—with a weak backhand. So was Yvon Petra. Bob Falkenburg won at Wimbledon—he had a weak forehand. Their compensating strengths were determination, concentration, and confidence—and, in Patty's case, a brilliant lob and an excellent serve. Developing the mental side of tennis (and maybe a bread-and-butter shot or two) should not be considered something unrelated to playing skill.

Nate Ritzenberg ranked number one in the Men's 55 Singles in Florida in 1977, and for a number of years has ranked in the top twenty nationally in his age group. I recently spoke with Nate at the Lakewood Country Club Seniors Invitational Tennis Tournament and asked him, "How do you become a champion?" He replied, "To be a champion you must grow up like Frank Parker. When Parker practiced, he took it seriously—there was no fooling around. In a tournament, even if he was ahead 5–0, 40–0, he continued to play with concentration, accuracy, precision, determination, and confidence. If you want to be a champion, you don't fool around. You can't play serious tennis for ten minutes, and then horse around for the next ten. Like Parker, you must have an obsession with winning, and feel real bad when you lose."

I had heard of Parker, and what Nate Ritzenberg said to me sent me off in search of more information about him. I found what I was looking for in a back issue of the *Milwaukee Journal*. In 1926, when Frank Parker was ten, he was shy, small, and spindle-legged. He played a little tennis, using not a racket but a paddle made out of a shingle. He shagged tennis balls at the Town Club on Farwell Avenue in Milwaukee. What little money he made he gave to his mother, a widow.

Around this time the *Journal* was sponsoring its annual Junior Tennis Tournament; 498 youngsters had entered, and the sponsor was hoping to make it 500. Frankie and a couple of

Billie Jean King played football and baseball in her early years and was spoken of as the All-American Tomboy. She was determined to be the best woman tennis player in the world, and put that goal before all others. She prepares for a match like the Wimbledon for months in advance by visualizing herself on the Center Court in the finals. She does not permit other thoughts to enter her consciousness. During the finals she blanks everything out but the point at hand. She has great confidence in her physical and mental ability to cope with the stresses of a match.

other boys who were batting a ball against the practice wall at the club were invited to enter, and they did. Parker did not last long in the tournament. The following year he entered the tournament and fared no better.

Observing all these youngsters was a man named Mercer Beasley, a teaching pro in the area, who remarked, "Look at all these kids just coming up. I'd like to take one of them—some kid just starting out, and without any bad playing habits—and mold him as you might mold, oh, anything. Too many pros don't know what they're doing. I'd like to take some kid who otherwise wouldn't have a chance." Young Parker happened to be around, and Beasley took him on, becoming in time a virtual father to him.

As a coach, Beasley emphasized seriousness and maximum concentration, and he instilled in his protégé determination and confidence. They worked long hours, almost every day, devoting a good portion of each practice to Parker's backhand, which would someday be one of the most potent in professional tennis.

The boy accepted the rigors imposed on him, which were alleviated with rewards, either verbal or tangible. Shyness, his most prominent personality trait, gave way to confidence, which was strengthened by his participating in the various tournaments Beasley entered him in: the Tri-State, the Western, the National Boys', the National Junior, and a number of state tournaments.

Frank Parker was ranked among America's top ten players seventeen times—a record of consistent success unmatched by Tilden, Johnson, Budge, or anyone else. He played on five Davis Cup teams, won the National Clay Court Championship five times, and the French championship twice.

Developing the qualities that made Parker's career what it was is our concern in the chapters that follow.

Chapter 2

How to Develop Determination

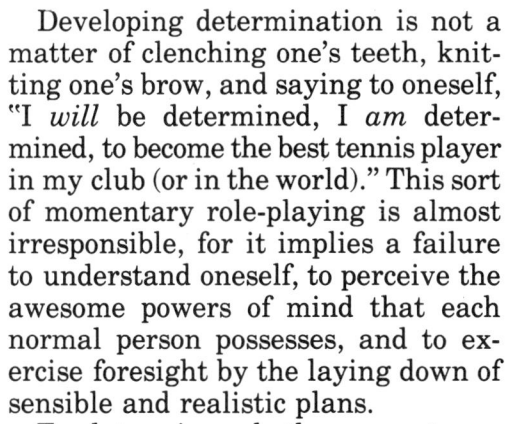

Developing determination is not a matter of clenching one's teeth, knitting one's brow, and saying to oneself, "I *will* be determined, I *am* determined, to become the best tennis player in my club (or in the world)." This sort of momentary role-playing is almost irresponsible, for it implies a failure to understand oneself, to perceive the awesome powers of mind that each normal person possesses, and to exercise foresight by the laying down of sensible and realistic plans.

To determine whether or not you are capable of developing determination, answer these questions:

    1. Have you ever been so caught up in a pleasant daydream or fantasy that the "real" world around you was, at least for a moment or so, blotted out?

    2. Have you ever noticed that when a person has acquired an interest in something, very often that interest becomes *active:* the person starts to learn more about the object of his interest, makes it a hobby, maybe even seeks to build a career around it—in brief, *does something?*

    3. Has it ever been your experience that some task which seemed hopelessly difficult or complicated or beyond your powers turned out to be "not so bad after all," maybe even manageable, once you had forced yourself to *start on it?*

If you've answered "yes" to these questions, then you can answer "yes" to the question whether you can develop the determination that leads to high-caliber tennis play. A "yes" answer to the first question indicates that you have a normally functioning imagination—a tremendously potent mental power (and one whose cultivation our world does little to encourage). A "yes" answer to the second question indicates that you can perceive the "pulling power" of something outside yourself—an interest,

Arthur Ashe is one of the most dynamic players in the history of the game. He cracks his lean, six-one, 154-pound frame into the ball with extraordinary power. As a youngster he was skinny and had to compensate by hard work to develop his tennis ability. Also, he was handicapped by being a black man at a time when tennis was dominated by whites. Determined not to let this stand in his way, he was spurred on to become one of the superstars of tennis.

an object, a goal—that ordinarily appears to possess no force or life of its own. Once you recognize that a thing—for us, tennis—has the power to draw and pull you to it, you can open yourself up to that power and make it a most helpful ally. If you answered "yes" to the third question, you have experienced the old truth that a little willpower can indeed go a long way, and you've experienced the sometimes funny and sometimes embarrassing but always instructive fact that we don't always see things as they are: we exaggerate their difficulties, their complexities, and in this way we make manageable things that seem unmanageable. Such experiences are ever-present allies—we need merely muster them.

Before we consider activities you can undertake and factors you can cultivate to develop the determination you need for superior tennis, it is necessary to understand that the matters we have just touched on must be given their due. It is not enough to acknowledge the role of the imagination, the pulling power of a goal or interest, the motive (or "pushing") power of the will, or the capacity of experience to alter our perceptions. These things must be allowed to enter into an ongoing process of self-understanding.

A kind of humility is called for. You must admit that such nonphysical forces operate on and manipulate you whether you like it or not, and that they largely determine who you are and what you can do. To admit this can be humbling. You may feel as if your self-image has been reduced to that of a puppet. But the admission brings with it a liberating reward: if you feel like a puppet, you can nevertheless see the strings and you can pull them yourself.

The very best tennis players have time and again said things implying that they had made such an admission and had turned the truths about themselves to their own advantage.

Clark Graebner has had a distinguished tennis career. He holds nine United States titles and has also won impressive international victories. He always worked hard and played best when concentrating intensely. Clark now divides his time between tournament tennis and his work for a paper company.

During the 1973 Palmetto Tennis Classic, held at the Carolina Coliseum in Columbia, South Carolina, I interviewed most of the sixteen contestants, among them John Newcombe, Clark Graebner, Raz Reid, Harold Solomon, and Dick Stockton. Many of their remarks indicated that they recognized the power of the nonphysical to affect them and their physical efforts, and that they had allowed it to work for the benefit of their game. Graebner, for example, remarked, "Money plus the national publicity I get are my main reasons for playing.... I have developed a reputation as being ranked among the first ten, and people expect me to win." He seemed to know that being conscious of goals ("money...publicity") and alert to perceptions ("people expect me to win") maintained his determination and hence his level of play. Somehow, predictions about Graebner tend to become actualities. If he is responsive to positive expectations, it is because he knows enough about himself to remain open to them. Similarly, Raz Reid said, "I'll make more money if I beat my opponent"—*purpose, induced determination*. "I look on this game as a position, like trying to get ahead"—*imagination*. "The better you are as a player, the more you are needed; and the more you are needed, the better you feel"—so, Raz, pick up the racket and go out there and win, because you've made yourself *determined to win*.

For champions, developing and maintaining a high level of determination is a never-ending responsibility. It is not something they leave behind when they advance beyond the novice or amateur stage of tennis. In particular, after poor play or a defeat, the true competitor exercises his determination by going over his mistakes and working harder than ever to get rid of a shortcoming. When "Big Bill" Tilden was twenty-seven years old, "Little Bill" Johnston beat him in the 1919 National Singles final. It was Johnston's forehand that undid Tilden's chop-stroke backhand. Tilden, already great, might have resisted admitting that he had a weakness. But he didn't, and he devoted an entire winter "to hitting a million backhands." Johnston never again beat him in an important match.

The big challenge in tennis is not so much the tournament as the training. The determination so handsomely displayed by a player one serve from a championship is simply the most prominent testimony to the determination of a million backhands.

Activities to Develop Determination

1. Enter tournaments.

Tournament play develops determination because it puts you into circumstances where determination is inevitably evoked. Practicing and training, necessary as they are, cannot substitute for competition. The developing player should resist the temptation to shirk tournaments until he has mastered his game. There is no such thing as absolute mastery of all the skills tennis calls for. But there is such a thing as a mentality that pretends such mastery is possible and that it should be attained before one competes in public. Don't let that mentality develop.

To Harry Hopman, the Australian champion and, at one time or another, coach of Rod Laver, Fred Stolle, Tony Roche, Roy Emerson, and Ken Rosewall, "competition is everything." He runs a camp in Florida, and the youngsters he trains are said to believe that they will someday be champions. He emphasizes tournament play, the essence of competition, and a chief means whereby his charges develop determination. It may not be possible for you or your children to work with Hopman, but you can certainly act on a principle that he has had such success with.

2. Act determined before and during a match.

Acting determined, even if it is a pretense or mere role-playing, makes you feel determined. To feel determined is to be determined. How you act, then, will determine how you play and how your opponent feels and plays. By your facial expression, body carriage, gestures, and general bearing, let him know that you are determined to win, expect to win, will play to win—will win. If he isn't as aware as you of the effectiveness of *appear-*

Sven Davidson of Sweden is a smart competitor and one of the tennis Grand Masters. Among his many honors are the French and German singles championships and the Wimbledon doubles championship. The top senior player was voted Sweden's "best player ever" before the arrival of Bjorn Borg. Sven's energy is inexhaustible, and his fighting quality is widely known.

ing a certain way, you will win the psychological battle for supremacy of determination—a major victory in any war.

Tilden's manner of approach to a court was a declaration: "I am going to beat you." All of his gestures and mannerisms, as well as his poise, expressed determination, and he gave the impression of controlling the court from the moment he stepped onto it. His adage was "A player who won't be beaten can't be beaten." Our advice: appear to be such a player.

Some players seek to stoke their determination and steal their opponents' thunder by seizing the initiative right at the start of a match. I once played a fellow who swaggered onto the court, threw his racket to the ground, and commanded, "Call it for the serve!" When I won the coin toss, "You serve!" he said. "No," I said, "you serve. I elect to receive." Knowing how to generate determination prepares you to deflect it when it's directed against you.

3. Associate with a group of competitors.

We may not always have the opportunity to enter tournaments, but if we let tennis exert its drawing power on us, we should find ourselves in the company of kindred spirits—other players. Groups of such players—clubs, school teams, community teams, city teams, and so on—not only provide opportunities to engage in the competition so necessary for developing determination but also help us to keep tennis prominent in our minds. Associating off the court with someone who may have defeated you or whom you will be attempting to defeat in a few days keeps the juices of determination flowing.

Notice that this suggestion, like others in this book, requires nothing more than letting your interest be your ally and making a decision to do something—something that is easy and should prove pleasant.

4. Compete against yourself.

This way of developing determination requires capacities present in any normal mind: memory, imagination, ingenuity. Recollect your previous record, then try to surpass it. Recall some characteristic of your game in recent weeks, and try to better it. Use your imagination to devise short-term goals whose likelihood of attainment will spur you to start working toward them now. Is your serve flawed by poor placement or an inability to strike at your opponent's backhand or forehand at will? A little ingenuity can help. Get an inner tube, and use it to designate a target in the service area (on the center line where it connects with the service line, forehand corner, backhand corner). Keep a written record of how many serves out of, say, a hundred land in the target area—a written record because a physical ob-

Pam Shriver smashes a shot to Chris Evert during the 1978 U.S. Open Women's Singles Championships. The sixteen-year-old was defeated 7-5, 6-4.

ject, like a pad, and a mechanical operation, like penciling in your results, provide the tangibility needed to buttress determination.

When you compete against yourself, you must beware of making an enemy of yourself. Be alert to this danger. Besides being imaginative and ingenious, you must be intelligent.

5. Use controlled, incremental thinking.

Operating your mind is not unlike operating your body or a machine. A delicacy of feel is desirable. Just as we allow an automobile engine to warm up, and then accelerate gradually, shifting smoothly from first gear to second and from second to third, so we should control our minds, letting them progress by increments to intense, high-pitched activity. When you want to use your mind to the advantage of your game, begin by opening it up to the prospect of a possible victory and the good feelings that will accompany one. Then consider that if there will be only one player on your side of the net, there will be only one player on the other side; considering that fact alone, your chances are 50–50. But maybe they're better than that. Picture yourself getting that first serve in . . . hitting deep forehands . . . and backhands . . . and volleying effectively at the net. Re-create the pleasant feelings that attended your last good game. As your mind, filled with positive images, progresses in this fashion, you are constructing a frame of mind for victory. And you can be sure that your game is played as much within a frame of mind as on a court.

If negative thoughts or images impinge on your progression of thought, force them away. Respond to a negative with a positive. If the prospect of defeat presents itself, recall the fact of a past victory. If your opponent's abilities insist that you grant them recognition, answer them with the thought of your own, or of the strategies you will encounter them with, or of the praise you have received in the past and will no doubt receive in the future, preferably the future that begins immediately after you have beaten your opponent.

6. Withstand adverse conditions.

It is human nature to discover laws and principles that explain why things turn out for us as they do. And it is a weakness of ours to sometimes assign to things a power over us in order to explain away some failure or disability. Athletes are especially inclined to develop superstitions and mind-sets about things that enter into the circumstances of a contest. In the case of tennis, players have been known to hold as an article of faith that they can't play in hot weather, or that they can't play in wind, or that they can't play with wooden rackets, or with yellow balls, or on clay courts: if they've decided they can't—they can't. To resist such negativism, it is first necessary to concede that one is prone to it and to be alert to its infiltrating one's game. Then action is called for. As often as possible, expose yourself to the conditions or deal with the things that you believe have or could have not necessary to do this in matches that count; it is probably wise to reserve practices for deliberately playing in bad weather or with equipment to which you are unaccustomed. Doing this sort of thing not only forestalls superstitions and fetishes but also develops the general mental toughness that ultimately is expressed in the determination seen on the face of a player about to win the big one.

7. Endure discomfort, stress, and disappointment.

This advice would be a belaboring of the obvious were it not for the fact that most of the readers of this book (as well as the author) have been conditioned to regard comfort as a norm of life, and something to be advanced in all the circumstances of our daily lives. Thus we want devices that remove the drudgery from housework, and cars that not only eliminate the necessity of walking but also offer a total-comfort environment in a climate-controlled driver's module. We all know that there once was a time when enduring discomfort—heavy labor, privation, the wind and the rain—was an accepted part of life. But serious tennis players should be aware that such a time still exists—for them. The advice, then, is to keep in mind that hardships are among the "givens" in the world of tennis. They are to be overcome by being accepted. Consciously accepting them will probably cause you to be a bit proud of yourself, of your hardiness. Such self-esteem props up and helps maintain determination.

If you examine the records of most outstanding men and women tennis players, you will be convinced that those who have attained success are those who have adopted the habit of accepting defeat and adversities as spurs to more and better-planned action. The player who loses but still fights on usually taps a well of mental energy that enables him to convert temporary defeat into permanent success. The tennis player who quits in the face of defeat never gets anywhere in tennis. He is unable to reach inside himself for strength during moments of distress, and he lacks hope and the will to succeed. Hope is strength in the present and it is preparation for the future.

Richard (Pancho) Gonzales exemplifies purposefulness, hope, and determination. With all his natural attributes, he still had to overcome one obstacle after another to reach the top—a tribute to his fighting spirit. He was enthusiastic and seemingly tireless in learning the game. He practiced hard and patiently with anyone who would hit the ball back to him. Darkness was the only opponent that drove him off a court. In his burning desire to be the best, he let his schoolwork lapse and he found himself in scholastic difficulties. This resulted in a two-year suspension from tournament play. Undiscouraged, Gonzales practiced all the harder, more determined than ever to get to the top. His willpower showed up clearly in the title match for the National Singles in 1949. He was to meet Ted Schroeder in the finals. The experts felt that Gonzales could never beat Schroeder. Gonzales lost the first two sets, 16–18 and 6–8, and most of the crowd felt he was through. They hadn't counted on the big kid's willpower, however, and he came back to win the next three sets 6–1, 6–2, 6–4.

On June 25, 1969, he beat Charles Pasarell on the Centre Court of Wimbledon in the longest match ever played there: 22–24, 1–6, 16–14, 6–3, 11–9. The match took five hours and twelve minutes. He played Torben Ulrich in the finals of the Almaden Grand Masters Tennis Tour in November 1976 at the Seabrook Island Club in South Carolina. In one of the long rallies that he lost, Pancho rebuked himself out loud, "You are an old man, you are lame, you are tired, but you're not dead," and he went on fighting to the end.

Francisco (Pancho) Segura is another example of a player who developed a strong willpower and overcame obstacles. Born of poor parents, weak and spindle-legged, and derided by playmates who called him "parrot foot," Segura had a drab future to look forward to. He had learned early in life to live with adversity, and as he gained stature as a tennis player it was nothing for him to have to spot his opponents five to eight inches in height and reach. Pancho has always had to give way to his opponents in the physical endowments that are associated with tennis players because he was not blessed with any to begin with. He just took what he had and set out to do the best that he could with it. All his life he has battled one handicap after another. Perhaps that is why fight is second nature to him. He started fighting at an early age, and his first, lonely battle was against sickliness.

Arthur Ashe overcame a different type of handicap: racial discrimination and feelings of inferiority. He has that great athletic asset—the one that separates the champs from the rest: the killer instinct. He had to fight his way up, and he still says, "I give it all I've got." Dr. Walter Johnson, an old coach and friend, said of him, "He was the youngest in the group and so skinny he looked like he had rickets. He was not as good or as natural as many of the others, but he was quick, he had fast eyes, and he always worked harder." Youthful feelings of inferi-

Today, at 50, Pancho Gonzales is still winning. Very aggressive and tremendously self-confident, he is still the mean and hungry player he was at nineteen. His unsurpassable determination and competitive spirit make him one of the most mentally tough players in tennis history.

ority and the determination to compensate for them may well account for Ashe's drive to win. After winning the first U.S. Open Tennis Tournament in 1968, in which the world's best players were entered, both pro and amateur, Ashe conceded that most of his life he had been spoiled. He added, "My father always sheltered me.... There were places we couldn't go, but we just accepted it. Now I realize that has a deep effect. You grow up thinking you're inferior and you're never quite sure of yourself." So you fight all the harder.

8. Keep your goal in the forefront of your mind.

Self-discipline, which everyone admires, and which is of inestimable importance in the development of a first-rate tennis player, is largely a matter of fixing your mind on a clear-cut purpose. Call it victory—or being the best. What matters is that you keep it prominent by making it concrete, by picturing it in the form of victory in your next local tournament or in a regional or national tournament you hope to participate in someday. Our minds require such concrete representations if they are to cling to something that is otherwise an abstraction, as easily blown away as a vapor. If you can keep your purpose vividly present in your mind, it will exert its power to draw you and your actions to it, and it will make the acquisition of self-discipline, a likelihood.

Here is Billie Jean King on goals, self-discipline, and related issues: "I need specific goals to get me going. I hate drilling, I hate anything repetitious, but I know that's what it takes for me to play well. I have to hit 250 crosscourt forehands every day, 250 down-the-lines. That's not creative to me—hitting the same shot thousands of times—but that's what I've got to do. *If I have a goal in mind, like to win at Wimbledon, that's all that I think about when I'm going through the repetition* [italics added].... Whatever your level of ability is—dammit, go for it! What irritates me is that most of the women don't work very hard. They don't get totally involved in the sport. They should read history books on it, know every old player, understand why tennis is where it is today. They should have a sense of history. Maybe they should do ballet, because it teaches you to keep your leg over your foot so you don't have injuries. They should keep their weight down, learn about nutrition. They should be artists. An artist is totally and intelligently involved in what he does. I don't think I would characterize most of the professional tennis players, men or women, as artists. They're part-time artists, and that doesn't work. That's why they're no better."

9. Develop enthusiasm.

Another spur to determination is enthusiasm. Enthusiasm can be powerful. It is the instrument by which failures and defeats can be transformed into a mental force promoting future successes and triumphs. The death of a dear friend or a loved one need not merely bring sorrow; it can serve as an inspiration to nobler efforts. A negative emotion can be changed into a positive one. Controlled enthusiasm takes the drudgery out of labor and inspires self-confidence.

How do you develop enthusiasm in tennis? There must be a desire to win. Let the desire become a burning desire. Fan it, coax it, and let it fuel your efforts. Take it to bed with you at night and get up with it in the morning. Write out a statement of your goal and the plan by which you hope to attain it. Follow the plan in your match with a persistence rooted in all the enthusiasm you can muster. Remember that a weak plan persistently applied is better than a strong plan applied intermittently or without enthusiasm. Keep away from those who are pessimists and discourage you. Their influence is deadening. Instead, associate with those who are optimistic about your winning. If you are following a course of action against your opponent, and find it is not working, change your plan but do not change your purpose. Keep your mind sold in the belief that you *will* win. Keep your mind positive at all times and remember that enthusiasm thrives only on a positive attitude.

The right attitude for a determined tennis player is expressed in these spirited lines.

> *If you think you are beaten, you are.*
> *If you think you dare not, you don't.*
> *If you'd like to win but you think you can't,*
>   *It's almost a cinch that you won't.*
> *If you think you'll lose, you're lost.*
>   *For out in the world you'll find*
>   *Success begins with a fellow's will—*
>   *It's all in the state of mind.*
> *If you think you're outclassed, you are;*
>   *You've got to think high to rise.*
>   *You've got to be sure of yourself before*
>   *You can ever win a prize.*
> *Life's battles don't always go*
>   *To the stronger or faster man,*
>   *But soon or late the man who wins*
>   *Is the man who thinks he can.*

Factors That Affect Determination

1. The influence of the family.

Personality traits present during one's early years tend to persist throughout life. Medorah E. Smith studied siblings from a number of families as children and as adults, and concluded that the traits of adulthood were consistent with the traits of childhood. Determination, Smith noted, was among the more unvarying ones. His findings are in harmony with Freud's belief that personality is largely fixed during the first five or six years of life. Genetic endowments and parental influence on the very young have, no doubt, a bearing on the development of athletes.

If you are a parent hoping to develop your child or children for tennis, expressions of approval and affection should greet each accomplishment, such as learning to bounce a tennis ball or swing a racket.

J. Donald Budge seems to have inherited his competitive spirit and determination from his Scottish father, who played soccer for the Glasgow Rangers. He took young Donald to soccer games on Sunday and, as manager of a local baseball team, exposed him to baseball. Don's first enthusiasm was baseball, but he grudgingly gave it up for tennis. His early baseball days may have been instrumental in his developing one of the finest backhands in tennis. He has a great deal of the lefty in him, perhaps because he batted left-handed. Don's brother Lloyd also contributed to his development. Lloyd was the number-one tennis player on the University of California team. Unable to find enough competitors of his age, he induced young Don to play with him and later encouraged him to enter tournaments. It is hard to imagine Budge's having the career that he had without such early influences.

2. The influence of a competition-minded, stimulating coach or friend.

There are plenty of coaches and instructors for developing tennis players nowadays. If you are still new to the sport, spend some time investigating them. Get as many opinions as you can about each one in your area, and do your best to judge the astuteness of those offering opinions. Give serious consideration to those coaches and instructors who are reputed to be

Don Budge was king of the tennis world from 1936 to 1946. The big redhead, known as "Mr. Tennis," had one of the best backhands in tennis history. Even when far behind, he never gave up. Outstanding determination, concentration, and confidence are required to win any *one* of the major world tournaments. In 1938 Don Budge won the Big Four: the national singles championships of Australia, France, Great Britain, and the United States.

not only knowledgeable and informative but also competition-minded and stimulating. The novice should be aware that he may be inclined to go easy on himself by choosing a mentor who will instruct him without pushing him. Such a novice should at least ask himself whether a pushy, high-powered mentor isn't just what he needs.

As for tennis partners, do what you can to find those who will challenge your abilities and make tennis exhilarating. You don't want to abandon friends merely because you've surpassed them in a sport, and you don't want to jeopardize your development by whiling away court time with an easygoing companion whom you can beat without moistening your brow. The development of mental toughness sometimes demands the exercise of mental dexterity—i.e. the dexterity that finds a way through conflicting interests and responsibilities.

3. Positive and negative reinforcers.

Bill Tym, a veteran of twenty years of national and international play, and ranked fifth nationally in Men's 35 Singles in 1975, recommends behavior-modification coaching to increase determination in tennis players. Goals have an important effect on a tennis player's output, and he suggests that a goal be established for each player. For example, a goal might be to hit at least twenty-five shots from the base line to a target area down the line. During this practice period the player must do his best in running and going after every ball. If the player does not cooperate in such an assignment, he is temporarily excluded from the group—a negative reinforcer. The player who attains the assigned goal is praised verbally or rewarded in some way—a positive reinforcer. Both kinds of reinforcers can greatly influence behavior. Positive reinforcers inform one that he is doing something correctly and encourage the continuation of the correctly executed activity. The coach need not reinforce every good stroke, but certainly frequent "rewards" will help to sustain motivation and improve performance. Success raises one's level of aspiration. Hence, the tennis coach should try to devise practice situations that tend to favor successes. Developing players would do well to seek coaching and training from those who resort to reinforcers and to other

Rosie Casals, a dynamic five-foot two-inch Californian, has been ranked among the first ten women players in the United States. She compensates for her small size by tremendous determination and confidence.

methods in accordance with what the psychologists have demonstrated about the workings of the psyche. They should also serve as their own sources of positive and negative reinforcers in frank and honest self-praise and self-criticism.

4. Situation factors.

Sudden occurrences before or during a match may evoke a powerful response in a player. An insult or unfair conduct on the part of an opponent, mistaken or questionable seeding—anything that touches one's self-esteem, reputation or ability to perform—may be a situational factor that can either help or hurt a player. The mentally tough and disciplined competitor will be prepared for such an eventuality and will exploit it as fully as possible. He will, of course, have a consciousness of the mental part of his game that will allow him to control his response. He will let the insult or injury arouse him enough to intensify his efforts and heighten his determination, but he will not let it ride roughshod over his self-control.

The pertinent advice, then, is to be aware that situational factors exist, that they can make or break your performance, and that planning how you will deal with whichever of them may come about should enable you to turn them to your advantage. Your plans should be solidly grounded in self-knowledge—an honest, undeluded assessment of yourself that can be verified by a review of your experiences in competitive play.

Chapter 3

How to Improve Concentration

Just about all good tennis players would agree that concentration—the exclusive and persistent attention to what you are doing and the exclusion of irrelevant thoughts and emotions—is of the utmost importance to winning tennis. When concentration is at its most intense, a kind of loss of self takes place: one's self becomes so engrossed in an object or activity that it is, in effect, inseparable from it. In the case of many activities—tennis among them—such concentration is necessary for maximum performance. Certainly such outstanding players as Budge, Seixas, and Kramer owed their great success in large part to their ability to concentrate.

Like determination, concentration demands more than a mere acknowledgment of its importance and more than a superficial adherence to a slogan, such as "Keep your eye on the ball." But since tennis centers on a ball and what one does with it, let's consider the advice "Keep your eye on the ball" and look into this form of concentration. The first thing an honest recollection of your tennis play should reveal about keeping your eye on the ball is that doing so isn't easy. How many players, especially beginners, can really watch the ball as it strikes and then leaves an opponent's racket, as it hits the ground on their own side of the net, as it bounces up and meets the strings of the racket? How many really see the spin of the ball, the trajectory of its flight, the behavior of its bounce? The answer to these questions can be gathered from all the wood shots and other miss-hits that every player has seen and no doubt made himself.

The virtual impossibility of keeping your eye on the ball completely suggests the virtual impossibility of developing perfect concentration. But you can try to approach it. It is said that before a match Billie Jean King will stare at a ball, concentrating on it and trying to put everything else

25

out of her mind. The player who thus attempts to establish a oneness with the ball can increase his ability to resist distractions.

Of course, concentration should embrace all aspects of one's game—for example, where your opponent is winning points and where you are losing them, how your backhand is faring against his serve, how successful your lobs have been, what weaknesses have been revealed in your opponent's game. Your concentration could well turn the game around. In the finals of the United States Indoor Championship in Philadelphia in 1977 such concentration had an important bearing on the outcome of the match. Connors was playing Stockton, and he hit his first eight smashes to Stockton's backhand. On each one, Stockton was moving the wrong way. But eventually his concentration enabled him to discern the pattern behind Connor's play and he went on to win the match.

One can look to the pros for examples of the kind of activity that leads to heightened on-the-court concentration. King, before she faced Evert on Centre Court at Wimbledon in 1973, spent days sharpening her concentration. Months before the match she would envision herself on Centre Court in the finals. These imaginings became a daily ritual. She would, in her imagination, experience the match—what it would feel like playing in it; its sensations; her performance, stroke by stroke; her analysis of her performance and of Evert's. Inevitably, matters other than tennis were pushed aside. On the day of the match she walked across the court toward the umpire's chair, her racket twirling, her attention on the crowd. Then, with play about to begin: "With all my heart I tried to blank everything out and concentrate on the match."

Evert avoids people on the day of a big match. Her mind fills with what is to come, so that when she steps onto the court, internal distractions cannot weaken her concentration. She is "psyched up."

Chris Evert Lloyd's two-handed backhand is a natural attacking weapon. Consistency is her chief trait; she developed it through strong willpower, excellent concentration, and confidence. She says, "Consistency is the foundation of good tennis." Chris Evert has grit, mental toughness, and determination. "She concentrates to the last point," says Margaret Court. "Even when she is losing she concentrates and doesn't give up."

A tennis player rarely maintains deep concentration for very long. Rather, the intensity and depth of his concentration fluctuates, and in any given match one player's potential for concentration will be greater than the other's. If we can imagine concentration potential as measurable by percentages, we can imagine a player stepping onto the court with a concentration potential as low as 5 percent (no player is absolutely devoid of the ability to concentrate) and his opponent stepping onto the court with one as high as, say 95 percent (nobody is capable of 100 percent concentration). The first player is the one who did nothing to prepare for the match. He is probably not especially interested in tennis. It may be that he is now playing only because he was talked into doing so. He may be angry because the match was scheduled at a time inconvenient for him. During play, peripheral sights and sounds distract him. He cares little about winning and he doesn't remember the score. He is happy when the match is over. In contrast to him, his opponent has spent a great deal of time preparing for this match. He may have already played it in his imagination and felt the satisfaction and elation of victory. He intensifies his interest in tennis by reading magazines on it. He has established goals for himself that give each match a meaning beyond the immediate one of his having played well and won or his having played badly and lost. He practices and trains daily. If this match carries a prize, his concentration embraces it. During play, distractions are powerless to infiltrate his mind, which is focused on what he is doing. Like his opponent, he is happy when the match is over—but for a different reason.

These two players are, of course, part of a fiction, but the fiction is true, because the concentration a player exhibits on the court is the result of a multifaceted process that may have begun years before. Among the elements of the process are motivation, interest, and goals.

Setting up and pursuing goals demands effort, and one aspect of concentration requires effort. You will want to establish short-term, intermediate, and long-range goals. A typical short-term goal would be to improve one of your less-developed strokes or to increase the percentage of your first serves that go in. The time limit for such a goal might be several weeks. Your immediate goal could be to win the tennis tournament sponsored by your community this year. A long-range goal might be to win the state or regional tournament—or even a national or world championship.

Closely linked to goals is motivation: goals draw us to them; motivation pushes or drives us. But motivation is something of a mystery. Who can know for sure what accounted for the motivation behind Chris Evert's once winning more than 100 consecutive matches or what accounts for the motivation behind Jimmy Connors' continuing to move through tennis like a juggernaut, no matter how tough the competition gets. It seems, however, that establishing goals activates motive power, and motivation and the pursuit of goals work together to improve concentration.

In the preceding chapter we remarked on the power latent in an object of interest and on how that power can serve as an ally in our efforts. If tennis is your interest, it makes sense to cultivate it on the court as well as off. Watching tennis matches, reading tennis magazines, and associating with tennis players are obvious ways of doing so. But the determined player should be aware that there exists a tendency among those who practice a sport to become somewhat lax in cultivating their interest off the court or off any field of play. Perhaps they suppose that their active participation renders other kinds of participation unnecessary. But why disregard anything that can aid us in what we are involved in? Parents who seek to cultivate a child's interest in tennis should, besides being encouraging and making tennis fun, tell him or her stories about tennis and tennis players and make books and magazines on the sport available. If possible, they should play tennis with the child. If they can't, they should seek out other youngsters with whom their own can play the game. The livelier and fuller a player's interest in tennis is, the more focused and tenacious his concentration during a match is likely to be.

One of the more immediate parts of the process of concentration may be called "getting your house in order." In anticipation of a tournament, make a list of all the equipment and supplies

Great Britain's Roger Taylor doesn't just look good. He has one of the best serves in tennis and brings great determination and aggressiveness to his game. Roger has been an exciting and brilliant player despite occasional lapses in concentration.

you will need: surgical gauze, for wrapping the handle of your racket in case it should get slippery; insecticide, in case a cloud of gnats threatens to descend on you; towels; a hat with a sun visor; extra wrist bands; salt; ice and water in insulated containers; an extra racket, and so on. You don't want your concentration to flag because you are nagged by a problem in the mere paraphernalia of the sport. Getting your house in order may embrace more than equipment and supplies. As Dell Sylvia—a Knoxville Racquet Club pro and a National 45 Grass and Clay Courts Champion, in 1975—says, "When I enter a national tournament, my wife pinch-hits for me on the job and my secretary takes on increased responsibilities; a tournament director takes care of the tournaments at the club and my maintenance man takes care of the tennis courts there."

Sylvia has also remarked on the connection between training and concentration: "Players spend a great deal of time on the physical or mechanical aspects of stroking. You must work on and expand your concentration ability when you practice. For example, when you are practicing your serve for fifteen minutes, put your whole mind into the effort. Take this practice seriously; do not let your mind wander. The next time you practice your serve, extend your period of concentration to twenty minutes, or even longer. Stretch your mind. Some players cannot concentrate that long, but if you want to be a champion, you must learn to concentrate for extended periods. When you practice with someone, try to discover those factors that enhance or hinder your concentration."

Similar advice comes from Marty Riessen, who has said, "Concentration can be improved through training. Practice a half hour daily on a particular shot, and concentrate on it. When you are in a match, you'll do better with it." Guillermo Vilas also believes that training with an eye to sharpening concentration can help a player to deal with distractions such as those he encountered during the United States Open Tennis Championships at Forest Hills in 1976, when "the whole atmosphere is different—people walking in during points, screaming; linesmen calling shots and then looking at you, unsure of the call. You have to learn to concentrate in the midst of that."

As you develop your ability to concentrate, you will find your attention span increasing from a few minutes to perhaps an hour or more. You will begin to be able to see nothing but the ball and its contact with the racket. You will keep distractions out of your mind, and your style of play will alter to further increase concentration. When serving, for example, you may intuitively emulate Stan Smith, who, when he starts rushing his serves, will slowly walk up to the base line, take a couple of deep breaths, and then bounce the ball a number of times, thereby slowing himself down and focusing his concentration on how and where he will hit the ball. You will also find that you are achieving greater stroke consistency, and that you are better able to sustain a rally—the two fundamental causes of short rallies are overhitting and a breakdown in concentration.

There will of course be times when your concentration will lapse, such as during the first game of a set following a long and difficult set that went to you. Keep in mind that intense concentration is fatiguing and breaks in play must be taken advantage of. During a break, give yourself over to deep breathing: think of your breath going in and out of your lungs; hear it passing through your nostrils. This will provide rest and leave you alert, relaxed, and will enable you to quickly regain concentration when you're on the court again. While you're on the sidelines, recall the good shots you made in the set that has just ended; review your mistakes; and decide what adjustments you will make.

Distractions

A distraction is a stimulus that causes a shift in attention and, if one is focusing attention on something, a reduction in concentration. It may be external or internal, momentary or prolonged, extremely disruptive of concentration or mildly so. Its duration and effect are partly due to the stimulus and partly to how distractible one is. Every tennis player is prone to distractions, in part because concentration, or resisting distractions, is a strenuous effort that cannot be maintained unflaggingly.

Concentration during a match entails assimilating such on-the-court matters as keeping your eye on the ball, deciding quickly what kind of shot to make, keeping the ball in play, and focusing on your opponent's play; demands eliminating internal and external off-the-court distractions. The player who maintains a high degree of concentration—that is to say, who endures the internal struggle between all the matters insisting on his attention—is necessarily postponing gratifications, for it is a kind of gratification to allow one's concentration to lapse. This calls for inner strength—self-control and willpower.

Distractions can be insidious. A while back, I was playing a friend at a club behind which are some cadet barracks. He was playing poorly. During the changeover he remarked how nice the music issuing from the barracks was. I hadn't noticed the music until he mentioned it, but he, obviously, had been pleasantly distracted by it, as the score—5–0, in favor of me—indicated.

For what it's worth, I would note that tennis players who are distracted as my partner was are not altogether unlike brain-damaged children distracted from some assigned task. A brain-damaged child will start on a task and then stop when a telephone in a nearby room starts ringing or some object—a car, a plane, a person—is glimpsed through a window. The person attending the child—somewhat like the tennis player who is oblivious of distracting phenomena until his opponent mentions them—remains unaware of the distraction until the child's behavior calls attention to it. Perhaps this comparison can help us to understand the mental forces involved in matches that are affected by, and perhaps turn on, distractions—like the one between Connors and Manuel Orantes for the United States Open in 1975. At one point in the match, Connors hit a forehand over the base line. Then, as he was changing courts with Orantes, a spectator—heard throughout the West Side Stadium—called out, "How much sleep did you get last night, chum?" Connors turned to him and gestured. Later in the match, Orantes' Spanish-speaking supporters distracted Connors (and became the recipients of another gesture). The match and the championship went to Orantes—a stunning upset.

Connors' opponents are sometimes the victims of distractions originating in his various movements, twitches, pluckings, and swayings—as, for instance, Jan Kodes was in the course of losing the quarterfinals of the U.S. Open in September 1976. Kodes' serve is a ritual consisting of a several-second-long suspension of movement, the bouncing of the ball, and the toss and smash. As Kodes went through it, Connors would spin his racket, hit the soles of his shoes with it, blow on his hands, pluck at his shirt, and sway. At times he would ape Kodes' service mannerisms. Kodes would delay his serve until Connors settled down and then, more than once, proceed to doublefault. Connors won the match in straight sets.

Three Types of Distractions

By definition a distraction has an effect on a person: no effect, no distraction. Thus, the wind, or some such stimulus, will be a distraction to one player and not to another. Distractions may be classified as external, internal, or external-internal. The external ones are caused by what can be seen, heard, touched, or smelled—an airplane overhead, a police siren, perspiration on one's racket grip, the

Even-tempered Manuel Orantes from Barcelona, Spain, came back from the dead in his semifinals match against Guillermo Vilas at the 1975 U.S. Open. He was down 6-4, 6-1, 2-6, and 5-0, but with courage and determination, he came back to win the fourth set 7-5 and the final set 6-4. The next day he crushed Jimmy Connors in the finals.

odors emanating from a nearby mill. Since such stimuli may be impossible to control, what matters is the player's reaction to them. The internal ones, though independent of stimuli outside the range of a player's control, may be more difficult to deal with. Worries, ongoing preoccupations, sudden recollections of duties or responsibilities, and little eruptions from the imagination, as well as on-the-court matters that are beside the point in regard to what a player should be immediately concerned with—all these can wreck one's game.

Top-ranked pros are not immune to them. In the 1975 U.S. Open at Forest Hills, in the third set of a match between Harold Solomon and Wojtek Fibak of Poland, the score was four games, apiece, love–15. Solomon dropped his serve at love. In the tenth game, Fibak won the first two points. Later, Solomon revealed that at these points he had been thinking about the plane trip home to Houston. As things turned out, he managed to dispel his thoughts of the flight, recover his concentration, and he went on to win, in a tie breaker.

External distractions may be linked with or may incite internal ones. In ordinary life it is a common experience for one to hear or see something, maybe only for a moment, that arouses his memory to intense and possibly prolonged activity. A person, for example, who has lived through a near-fatal plane crash might, for at least a moment, relive the experience when he sees or hears a plane overhead. His reliving it amounts to a distraction from the present, however slight and short-lived. An external-internal distraction may have been a significant factor in Roy Emerson's loss to John Newcombe in the quarterfinals of the 1970 Wimbledon. Emerson was ahead at the start of the fourth set when his shorts began to fall off (a button had popped). Newcombe laughed, the crowd laughed, and the match was halted until a safety pin came to the rescue of Emerson's modesty. But not of his game: he went on to lose. There is no point in conjecturing what may have been going on in his mind; it is enough to note that after his embarrassment his play fell off.

Handling External Distractions

There are many ways to handle external distractions. One way is to cut them out. Persons who have handled horses know the importance of sometimes placing blinders on them. In the past, horses pulled carts on streets, and without blinders they would be startled and distracted by passing traffic. Most cities had ordinances prescribing that horses wear blinders on city streets to avoid accidents. Don Budge has recommended the use of mental blinders to avoid distractions and maximize concentration. He advises tennis players never to look at an opponent when he is at net and they are on base line. He even recommends restricting peripheral vision. He has said that the less you see of your opponent during the match, the better off you are. Only when your

Manuel Santana of Spain is agile and has an excellent touch. Though he is quiet on the court, he fights for every point with extraordinary determination. He has a keen ability to concentrate.

opponent sends you a high lob that you let bounce do you have time to look around.

Perhaps the most important way of learning to handle external distractions is by practicing under various kinds of distracting conditions. Give yourself an opportunity to train for the various external distractions that may arise in a tournament. If your concentration is affected by the wind, welcome an opportunity to play in the wind. Expose yourself to visual and auditory distractions during practice play so that you will be used to the ones that may arise in tournament matches. For example, just outside the courts where I often play there are, at noon, invariably a number of teenagers who are loud and boisterous. Rather than look upon their distracting presence as a handicap, I have accepted it as a challenge to learn to live with auditory distractions.

Since the wind is a distraction and a troublesome annoyance for many players, we should devote some place to coping with it. (What follows implies that dispelling a distraction may involve much more than attention to the mental aspects of tennis.) One thing to do, of course, is to practice on windy days. Another thing is to know the kinds of wind that affect play, especially serves, the different ways they affect it, and the adjustments they necessitate. The wind can blow behind the server: when it does, the server needs to serve slices to prevent the ball from going out. It can blow against the server: under this condition, he must be careful not to overhit. It can blow across the court: here, adjustment in the serve is necessary to compensate for the distance that the wind will carry the ball in one direction or another. Besides these three kinds of wind there are many variations, such as the wind blowing from the right rear or left rear, or the right front or left front. There are gusty winds, which produce the most frustration: here the toss is particularly important. Guide the ball with the tossing hand as high as possible before releasing it, and reduce the height of the toss, to prevent the wind from interfering with hitting the ball squarely.

There are other measures that the player can take to cope more effectively when serving in the wind. First, it is important to have sufficient foreknowledge about the weather conditions. The weather report will be helpful, but it is best to get to the court well before the match to size up the weather conditions on the playing area. A report may indicate that the wind will be fairly strong, but on the court you may discover that it is blocked by a building or that it is bad on one part of the court and not on another.

Second, it is important to practice serving in the tennis-court area about an hour or so before the match to learn the wind conditions as it affects serves. This suggestion is in keeping with Soviet sport psychology. The Soviets make special psychological preparations for competition by reproducing the conditions of an upcoming contest and having their athletes train under them.

Third, once the match starts it is important to keep in mind that greater concentration is required on a windy than on a nonwindy court. When concentrating on serving, the server should be especially intent on how and where he is going to hit the ball.

Another psychological factor important in serving and playing in the wind is good frustration tolerance. The player who gets upset by the wind and shows his discomposure in his behavior toward his opponent beats himself. He should remember that his opponent is playing in the same wind. Anything that the server can do to relax himself should be done: bouncing the ball before serving, taking his time walking up to the base line to serve, looking at his opponent for a

Recently the Number One World Champion, Jimmy Connors has been playing tennis since he could walk. A protégé of Pancho Gonzales and Pancho Segura, he was groomed for championship play in the competitive Southern California arena. Gonzales later said about him, "He is a mean, vicious competitor." Connors asserts himself at the start of a match and constantly attacks. He has a hard serve and likes to fire bullets from the baseline. Ashe said about him, "I never played anybody who could keep up such tremendous groundstrokes for so long."

moment before serving, breathing deeply several times before starting the serving motion. At the United States Open Tennis Championships in 1976, Jimmy Connors took twenty-eight seconds from the end of one point to his serving for the next. He did a number of things during the twenty-eight seconds: he twirled his racket, hit the bottom of his shoes with it, pulled his shirt at the shoulder, blew on his hands, and bounced the ball several times.

Last, during the match the player should display adaptability to the wind condition. After discovering the bad effect of the wind on the serve, the server should try to make some adjustments.

Shadows or a blinding sun may be a serious external distraction. Whenever you have an opportunity to practice under such conditions, do so. Strong concentration is necessary when playing in shadows: you must keep your eye on the ball more intently than you usually do. A tennis hat with a sun visor may help you see the ball better when the sun is unusually intense. If you are forced to face the sun when serving, you may be able to see the ball better if you toss it to one or the other side of your regular toss. If this does not work, you might try changing your stance, either by standing somewhat sideways or by facing the net more directly than you usually do. With a little experimenting you can handle this distraction.

Some players are distracted by playing on a particular type of surface. They like clay courts better than hard-surfaced courts or vice versa. Play on different kinds of surfaces and adjust to all of them. Seek to develop the hardy attitude that you can play on anything. Some players have a phobia about playing with any other than their favorite brand of balls. They become distracted when playing with balls not to their liking. I have heard many such players complain that they lost only because they could not play with their favorite brand. Welcome the opportunity to play with and adjust to new and old balls of every variety and manufacture. Sometimes birds flying in the vicinity, gnats, or other objects distract players. If birds bother you, make up your mind that they never again will, and if you suspect that you'll be playing where gnats swarm, take along an insect repellent that works.

Spectators distract some players. If you are in a tournament and you want to win, forget the girl or, if you're a woman, a fellow in the gallery who is eying you. During practice play, accept the presence of spectators so that you can adjust to the ones who will be all around you during tournament play. Many players depend too much on one racket, and when a string snaps or the racket breaks, they feel no other one will do. Playing with a different one can be an external-internal distraction. Suggestion: have two or more rackets as nearly identical as possible and get comfortable with them by using them in practice. Heat can sometimes make you so uncomfortable that you get concerned about your well-being. Remember that your opponent is playing in the same heat and he too is affected by it. Get used to practicing in hot and humid weather and you will be prepared for whatever heat you encounter in tournament play. Fatigue can interfere with concentration. When you are exhausted, you may start to think more about your stamina than about your game. To avoid this distraction you need to be in good physical condition. Jimmy Connors lost to Dick Stockton in the finals of the National Indoors at Philadelphia in January 1977. John Newcombe, one of the TV commentators, ascribed Connors' loss in large part to his not having played in a five-set match for many months. Stockton, however, had just returned from Australia, where he had played in a number of four- and five-set matches in 90- and 100-degree heat. Taking deep breaths may help to reduce fatigue temporarily, but there is no substitute for good physical condition.

Handling Internal Distractions

Internal distractions may be more damaging to concentration than external ones. They tend to last longer, and while they work on you they remain hidden within you. If you are prone to them—and we all are—acknowledge that you are. Doing so is not only the first step to take but also one of the most potent measures that can be taken to dispel these distractions. When a distracting thought, memory, feeling, or concern enters one's consciousness, it becomes an exposed object, and therefore something with which one can deal. For instance, when you are consciously attending to, say, a business matter—shining the light of the mind on it, as it were—the business matter cannot be lurking in the dark and operating on you. In general, when we are agents operating on things that we have made into objects, the things cannot be agents operating on us. One can also put into writing the concerns that encroach on the mind when it has other things to attend to. Reducing something to words on paper makes it, in a sense, a smaller thing than it was.

When you are in a match, force yourself to think about how you will defeat your opponent. Should you take the net more often? Or lob more often? Or hit the ball deeper? And control your temper: losing it amounts to generating internal distractions. Throwing your racket or batting balls over the fence—any such outburst—ruins coordination, speed, and timing. Realize that you are going to get your share of bad and good breaks. Recall the many good or lucky shots that you made. In the long run, these even up with the bad shots that just missed the line or the lobs that the wind blew out. Concentrate on the present point. It is the next shot that counts. Since a poor shot undermines confidence and concentration, the best insurance against following one poor shot with another is to substitute a positive and constructive approach to the coming shot. Don't brood on what's past. Put in your mind such thoughts as "Keep your eye on the ball; hit the ball deep; put your first serve in." Excellent self-control was displayed by Bjorn Borg in the course of defeating Connors in the finals of the Grand Slam Tennis Tournament at Boca Raton, Florida, in January 1977. Borg had Connors at match point in the second of a three-set match. Connors hit a drop shot and was out of position for the return that Borg should have easily made. Borg hit the ball in the net. But he didn't let this bad shot unsettle his concentration. He lost the second set, but with even more determination and concentration he went on to beat Connors in the third set 6–2.

Frequently a player will lose concentration as a result of a bad call by his opponent. Instead of thinking about the next point, his mind gets stuck on the bad call. He is angry at his opponent; his resentment builds up. He may even forget his goal: to win. When you must endure a bad call, try to keep cool. If there is a flagrant violation on the call, tell your opponent about it and attempt to remedy the situation. If you think you are getting a raw deal, stop play and request a referee. Be fair and impartial yourself and believe that your opponent is the same. You and he make honest mistakes. At home, work out a philosophy in respect to bad calls; on the court, follow it.

If you can't recall the score, or if you don't remember who won or lost the last point, then you are internally distracted. You are like someone who is reading and aware that there are words in front of him but is unable to attend to what he sees. Should somebody ask him to tell what he has read, he is at a loss to do so. In tennis, as in reading, to have a high level of concentration you must be interested in what you are doing.

Handling External-Internal Distractions

Sometimes a distraction consists of both external and internal stimuli. You may be distracted by the antics and/or clowning of your opponent—an external distraction. You may be fur-

Nancy Richey Gunter is a serious, hard-working Texan. She has the most savage ground strokes in the game and powders the ball cleanly from side to side with better pace and more control than any other woman player except Chris Evert Lloyd. She practices constantly and is concentration personified on the court.

ther distracted by recalling an encounter with similar behavior in a previous match—an internal distraction. Thus, you are doubly distracted. Suffering external-internal distractions is a common experience of many who have competed with Ilie Nastase.

Ilie Nastase, nicknamed "Nasty," is notorious for his outbursts and childish antics. Some spectators adore him for them and disregard the poor sportsmanship they entail. Nastase dislikes linesmen and officials. He berates them, hurls balls and rackets at them, and embarrasses them. He quits in the middle of some tournaments and fails to show up for others.

In 1969, at Wimbledon, Nastase gets enraged at a linesman while playing Mark Cox in a Davis Cup match. He kicks chairs and stomps around the court. In 1971, at Nice, in a match with Jan Kodes, he complains about decisions, badgers officials, and threatens to quit the match. This behavior throws Kodes completely off his game, and Nastase wins. In 1972, in London, Clark Graebner is so provoked by Nastase's tactics that he goes over the net, jabs him in the chest, and berates him spiritedly. In 1973, at the Western Open in Cincinnati, while playing Manuel Orantes, Nastase curses the referee, refuses to resume play when instructed, and smashes balls at linesmen.

Nastase ignores the rules of tennis as his whims dictate. He feels he is doing nothing wrong and believes he is the victim of persecution by spectators and tournament officials. He is a master at distracting his opponents and upsets so many of them that they lose control of their emotions and of their game.

What is the best way to play a Nastase? How can you handle him so that his behavior does not upset or distract you?

One way to counter his misbehavior—a way that I shall describe but not recommend—is to plan an event during the match that will seriously distract him. I once observed a match that offers an example of the severe effects of planned distractions. A nationally known tennis coach, trying to gain national prominence for a local and relatively unknown tennis player, had invited a nationally known player to a match with his protégé. The coach had seen to it that strong-voiced and highly vocal boys would view the well-publicized match from a tree just outside the court. The boys knew the local player, and the coach knew that they would be strongly for him. During a critical point in the game, the boys began yelling, "You can't hit that ball,———" (they called the well-known player by his name). The crowd broke out in laughter and the national player was distracted. He double-faulted; his game fell apart; and the local unknown went on to win the match.

Another way of reacting to the behavior of a Nastase is to do what is natural for you. If you see him as a clown, then laughing at him may be your best tactic. Do whatever is comfortable and natural for you in the situation. If he does something that irritates you, then you may get angry at him, as long as your anger is under such good control that it doesn't overwhelm you and reduce your playing ability. The disadvantage of this tactic is that it is risky: controlled anger tends to become uncontrolled. In other words, the tactic can backfire. Not only that, but if you let his antics anger you, you are rewarding him, and he is likely to exploit your discomposure and provoke you even more and thus spoil your game even more. (This is what might have happened to Graebner in the aforementioned match.) This method, then, may work only for those players who have excellent emotional control. But there are not too many tennis players, or human beings generally for that matter, who have such emotional control that they will not become upset when placed in a situation comparable to that of playing "Nasty."

Hypnosis and self-hypnosis are other techniques that may be used to counter a Nastase. They are, however, extreme measures, and may not be necessary. I have used hypnosis, with varying degrees of success, on tennis players who sought to overcome such problems as a difficulty in maintaining concentration, an inability to keep their eyes on the ball, a lack of motivation, a tendency to get upset easily, and an inability to control anxiety.

When hypnosis is prescribed, the person who is planning to play someone like Nastase will be given such suggestions as: "You will concentrate on the ball at all times even though ——will try to distract you with his misbehavior; he may needle you and try to impress on you the notion that you are inferior to him, but you will not be influenced by this kind of talk. You know you are a better player than he. You have more skill. You will win. He will argue with officials and hit balls at linesmen, but you will understand that he is trying to distract you and you will concentrate on winning each point. . . ."

Ignoring bad behavior is another way of handling it. If a player who is prone to histrionics sees that you are not reacting to his performance, he will probably realize that he is expending energy uselessly and abusing his talents, and he himself may bring the curtain down. Like hams of the stage, hams of the tennis court wither and fade if they are without a responsive audience. This method of nonresponsiveness is used successfully by teachers against youngsters who act out in their classrooms.

Dick Stockton used the method successfully when he played, and beat, Nastase at Wimbledon. Nastase went into his act, taking an umbrella out of the stands and waiting to receive serve with the umbrella in one hand and his racket in the other. Stockton simply turned his back on Nastase and refused to be part of the star's audience. He later explained, "I've seen him disrupt too many matches and break too many players' concentration."

It is difficult to develop imperturbability, but it can be done, as the careers of many outstanding tennis players attest. Helen Wills Moody was known as "Little Miss Poker Face" because she displayed little emotion in competition. Her opponents were often disconcerted because they could not unsettle her. Donald Budge, the first to win the Grand Slam, was notable for his keen concentration and minimal distractibility. Frank Parker, twice National Singles champion and seventeen times ranked among the top ten, never questioned a call and hardly ever expressed any emotions on the court. He played as objectively as anyone possibly could, thanks, in part, to his coach, the late Mercer Beasley, who included in his training program the development of what he considered an "objective approach" to the game. He taught his students to accept with resignation linesmen's calls and to control their emotions completely. He believed that in any match the bad and the good calls will generally balance out. He instilled in his students (Parker, Ellsworth Vines, Doris Hart, among others) a most important virtue: that of playing tennis without being distracted by outside stimuli. Some believe that Beasley's instruction bordered on the excessively mechanical and that he tended to develop automatonlike players, but all will agree that his method worked.

One of the best ways of coping with distractions is to use the method of "selective inattention," a capacity first recognized by Harry Stack Sullivan, a prominent neo-Freudian. Selective inattention restricts what goes into your consciousness; it keeps certain things out altogether. It can therefore be a way of controlling, maybe even of dominating, situations that arouse anxiety. It works like this: you focus your attention only on what is appropriate—what is relevant and manageable—and ignore everything else, including any distractions that try to intrude into your consciousness. Thus, you perceive only part of a situation. When you are practicing selective inattention, you may notice potentially distracting stimuli, but you don't grant them admittance. At most, they remain on the periphery of your consciousness—a vantage point insufficient for them to disturb you.

On the court, the method would, for instance, require that you increase your concentration on the ball, and when you cannot look at or concentrate on the ball owing to, say, a melodrama that your opponent is starring in, you look at and concentrate on some other object, like your tennis racket, until the performance is over. If you are looking at and are concentrating on the ball or your tennis racket, you will be, at most, dimly aware of the disturbance. This method, I believe, is more effective than that of looking upon but refusing to react to a distraction because this method has you doing something at least minimally positive and constructive and concedes nothing, not even recognition, to that which is negative and destructive.

Not only may you encounter an opponent who distracts you externally and internally, but you may encounter a hostile crowd that will tax to the limit your concentration and frustration tolerance. In May 1978, Jose Higueras, of Spain, was facing Adriano Panatta, of Italy, in a semifinal match of the Italian Open Tennis Championship. Higueras had taken a commanding lead, having won the first set 6–0 and leading in the second 5–2, when the notorious "Lion's Pit"—the mercilessly partisan crowd, given to jeering and throwing things—swung into action. Encouraged by the crowd that sat through sunshine and rain, Panatta eventually found his mighty serves and deadly smashes and pulled into a 6–5 lead. At that point, the sixty-nine-year-old umpire, Bertie Bowron of Britain, ordered two more serves to Higueras, claiming that crowd noise had been responsible for a faulty serve Higueras had just made. But the umpire was overruled by referee Sergio Baruti, who ordered a single service. Bowron then announced, "At this point, I go." An Italian umpire replaced Bowron, and the set ended with Panatta winning 7–5. Higueras then walked off the court.

Bowron later said that the Italian referee had erred in overruling him. "If play is interrupted for any reason, you give two serves," Bowron said. "There is no way to play here," said Higueras, on his way from the court, as a boisterous crowd of close to 10,000 bade him farewell with calls of "clown, clown." A soft-drink can and a 100-lire coin were also hurled at him, but both missed. (The tossing of a 100-lire coin at someone is considered an insult in Italy.) Higueras afterward said, "It's important to win, but not if winning necessitates playing under these conditions. I want to win in a sportsmanlike manner. They called me every name you can imagine. I don't think I'll come back to Rome to play again." Veteran tennis experts said this was the first time that a player had walked away from play in a major tournament because of a hostile crowd.

Previous victims of the crowd and their hero, who was unseeded—second-seeded Vitas Gerulaitis, sixteenth-seeded Hank Pfister, and giant-killer Victor Amaya, all Americans—had complained that the crowd had unnerved them and declared that they could easily have won on a neutral court. Panatta, nervous and smoking a cigarette (as he usually does not) after the match, defended the Rome crowd, saying, "They get excited. Other players should know this and react accordingly. The Spanish crowd is no different."

The history of amateur and professional sports in recent years suggests that vicious disruptions, planned or unplanned, may become more frequent. Tennis players, and other athletes, must learn to guard against them, so that the planned distraction fails and your opponent suffers more than you do from it, whether it is of his or of his partisans' devising.

How to Check Your Concentration

How can you check on your concentration in a match? By looking for the indicators of distraction, among which are the following:
1. You don't know what the score is.
2. You can't recall how you won or lost the preceding several points.
3. You can't recall where you or your opponent served last.
4. You are interacting verbally with your opponent and the umpire more than you need to.
5. You are interacting with spectators.
6. You are brooding on the loss of critical points or what you see as a bad line call.
7. You are thinking of events that will occur after the match or that occurred prior to the match.

These are the signs that you are concentrating:
1. You have a feeling of being at one with the ball.
2. The ball and the match are presently the only things in your world.
3. You blot out of your mind irrelevant visual, auditory, and other stimuli, and focus exclusively on the play at hand.
4. You have no awareness of pain or fatigue or bodily discomfort.
5. You feel you've apprehended the patterns in your opponent's play and you know how to foil his tactics.
6. During time-outs you understand why your match has developed as it has, and you apply your understanding to devising a strategy for the part of the match to come.

Chapter 4

Anxiety and the Would-Be Winner

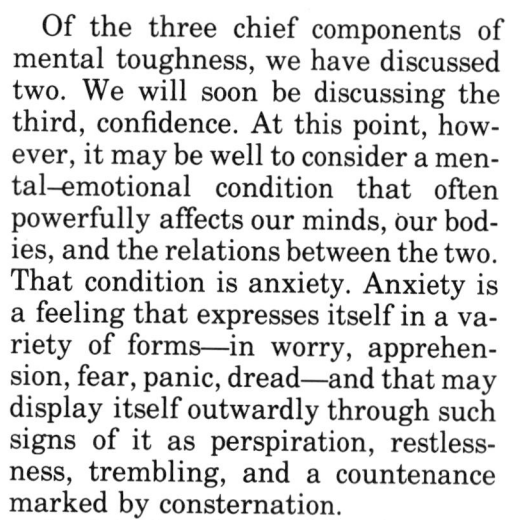

Of the three chief components of mental toughness, we have discussed two. We will soon be discussing the third, confidence. At this point, however, it may be well to consider a mental–emotional condition that often powerfully affects our minds, our bodies, and the relations between the two. That condition is anxiety. Anxiety is a feeling that expresses itself in a variety of forms—in worry, apprehension, fear, panic, dread—and that may display itself outwardly through such signs of it as perspiration, restlessness, trembling, and a countenance marked by consternation.

Anxiety is to be distinguished from fear. Fear is normally of something specific and known, whether it is physically present, such as a snarling dog or a man who appears to be a mugger, or present to the imagination, such as the prospect of driving on an icy road or facing an Internal Revenue Service auditor. Anxiety is *about* something in the sense that we know the circumstances in which something arouses the feelings that constitute our anxiety—a forthcoming public-speaking engagement, the responsibilities of our careers, or a tennis match in which we will face not only a tough opponent but the presence of spectators, an atmosphere electric with expectancy and the certainty that our performance will be assessed and perhaps widely commented on.

In certain situations, fear may give way to anxiety or anxiety to fear. If, for instance, you are driving and you suddenly see a car coming your way, in your lane, you are immediately fearful of it. If you swerve and manage to avoid it, and watch it recede in your mirror, you will, of course, feel relief, but you may—even though the danger is behind you and no danger is to be seen ahead—also feel considerable anxiety as you continue driving along. Yet there is no precipitant of your feelings—no specific something that has aroused them—and consequently your anxiety is vague, diffuse, and prospective. (Guilt, by contrast, is retrospective: it is aroused by a looking-back at something.)

Anxiety is pervasive. It can arise in connection with anything that is a part of one's life: one's schooling, career, marriage, wealth, possessions, recreations, or whatever. Its sources have been speculated on and written about by such prominent thinkers as Sigmund Freud, Erich Fromm, Karen Horney, Otto Rank, and Harry Stack Sullivan.* Among the sources of anxiety is one that is plainly observable—and relevant to the chief concern of this book. That source is our culture's apparent need to seek prestige through competition. From our earliest years onward we are enjoined to compete, to succeed—to compete so that we may succeed. Thus, if you win a tennis match you gain prestige, certainly in your own eyes and perhaps in the eyes of others. If you lose, you must struggle, if only a little, not to feel morose and self-embittered. Winning seems to certify our capacity for success. An opponent, then, is an obstacle not only to victory but to the host of good things that go with it. An opponent is inevitably at or near the center of a situation productive of anxiety.

Anxiety is normally unpleasant. Those who seem to quest for it, such as some mountain climbers or automobile racers, may be regarded as exceptional cases. But it is not always bad for us. In a moderate degree, it can make us alert to the wiles and tactics of an enemy—including, of course, the one on the other side of a net. Likewise, it can serve as an early-warning device, signaling a threat or a problem not yet perceived by the more sharp-focusing of the mind's receivers. And it can tap our adrenaline, call up our reserve powers, and heighten our abilities. In excess, anxiety throws off our physical coordination, disrupts and disorganizes our thinking, sabotages our actions, and, more generally, seems to overwhelm us.

The majority of us probably experience anxiety only to a moderate degree, the stresses of life affecting us pretty much the same. But there are those who experience pathological anxiety, which is more severe and persistent than what the rest of us experience and is occasioned by stresses that have little effect on most people. And there are those who experience anxiety only in situations that forebode catastrophe.

People under stress tend to revert to early learning experiences, forgetting more recently acquired knowledge. In an experiment designed to test the theory of regression under stress, two psychologists, Richard Barthol, of the University of California, and Nani D. Ku, of Pennsylvania State University, taught eighteen people first one and then another method of tying a bowline knot—a knot forming a loop that doesn't slip. Three days later the eighteen were put into a stressful situation and instructed to tie the knot. Sixteen of them used the method that they had been taught first. The psychologists' conclusion was that, when under stress, people resort to the first-learned methods that make for success or that are appropriate to a situation.

This reversion tendency may explain the alterations sometimes observable in the playing style of a player in a close, tense match: he is reverting to what he learned first. It is said that when Barry McKay took up tennis he first learned to hit hard. This would explain why, when he is behind in a match or is in a comparably stressful situation, he plays a hard-hitting game. An awareness of

---

*See, for instance, Freud's *Problem of Anxiety*, Fromm's *Escape from Freedom*, Horney's *Our Inner Conflicts*, Rank's *Trauma of Birth*, and Sullivan's *Conceptions of Modern Psychiatry*.

the reversion tendency is desirable both for beginning players and for their coaches. Some coaches believe that a beginner should first learn to hit hard and should later develop control and accuracy. Others—Mercer Beasley being a notable example—concentrate on developing accuracy in the beginner. Which of the two schools of thought is right is not the issue here. The point is that a player's early acquisitions of techniques and skills are likely to come to the fore when stress and anxiety attend his play.

The pattern of anxiety in tennis players facing stiff competition in important tournaments is rather like the pattern of anxiety in patients awaiting surgery, most of whom experience increasingly intense anxiety as the time of the operation approaches. Weeks before an important tournament, a player's emotions in regard to it are, typically, in a state that varies from slumber to moderate alertness. A few days before the tournament, his emotions and alertness will probably be heightened. Two days before it, they are further heightened and anxiety may be setting in. The night before the match, anxiety may be such as to prevent his sleeping.

On the day of an important tournament, a player's emotional state may be so intense as to unsettle him completely. Here is an account of my own experience during a period of time extending from an hour before a match in a recent city tournament to the end of play. One hour before the finals got under way I suffered pre-game jitters. I paced up and down the bedroom floor thinking about the big match. In an attempt to calm down, I tried to read the newspaper and a magazine, and then I turned on the TV, but I could not get involved in any of these things. I seemed on guard and keyed for action, and my bodily functions reflected my state. I had a hard time thinking coherently and exercising ordinary forethought. Simple things stymied me. For example, in changing from street to tennis clothes, I couldn't manage to hang up my street clothes properly and wound up throwing them on the bed and floor helter-skelter. My memory wasn't working well, either: I forgot my wrist band and my towel. I was irritable toward my wife, who (praise her) always anticipates, and does what she can to allay, her husband's wretchedness.

Before going on the tennis court one of my friends tipped me off to the need for an adjustment in my dress. I went to the tennis court with three tennis rackets and a large brown leather valise filled with insect repellent, salve to improve the grip, tennis balls, and other items. I was afraid to let my valise out of sight. I hoped that I would not "blow up" or "choke up" at the start of the match or, if I won, at the moment of victory. Play started. In serving, my arms seemed stiff, and I was wound up like a spring. There was tension in my legs and my chest and shoulders. I was confused, too: I was about to serve on the wrong side and I forgot the score in the second game.

Even though I had practiced my service for hours prior to this event, I choked and could not hit the ball accurately or with the power that I had hit it in practice. Luckily this choking lasted only a few minutes, during the beginning of the match, but I sensed it again when the score was one set apiece and four-all in games. Again I became tense and my serve suffered. I was lucky to win this match. After it was over, I asked my opponent to be frank and tell me how he had felt before and during the match. He told me that he had experienced feelings similar to mine. He said that he had become jittery two days before the match and the jitters had lasted until after the match. Even though he had lost, he was glad the match was over, because now he said he could sleep soundly again.

Such an experience is not peculiar

to amateurs. Rod Laver, as quoted by Arthur Daley in *World Tennis*, said this of a match he had played with Mark Cox at the British Hard Courts: "All of a sudden this had ceased to be a routine match. I felt as if I were carrying the entire burden of professional tennis on my shoulders. Cox was playing well, but not that well. I just had to win and it became an emotional experience—like playing for the Davis Cup or being on the Centre Court at Wimbledon or Forest Hills. The adrenaline began to flow and I gave it that little extra. I usually don't get nervous on the court, but I was nervous this time, because this had become an important match. The tension and the atmosphere of the first open tournament in history do strange things to a man, especially when this marked a new era in tennis." Laver beat Cox 6–4, 6–0, 6–1.

His feelings in this match notwithstanding, Laver is a prime example of a player with the ability of controlling anxiety. After one of his many notable triumphs he remarked, "Confidence is the thing in tennis—as I'm sure it is in any sport. I hear other athletes talk that way. Confidence separates athletes of similar ability."

Tennis players vary in the degree of jitters or anxiety they have when under stress. Some seem to remain composed under almost any circumstances; others get butterflies in their stomachs, under minimal stress. Tennis players, like people in general, can be classified as high- or low-anxiety types. There is evidence to indicate that a high-anxiety person under stress and pressure, such as that of a tennis tournament, is likely to perform less well than a low-anxiety person.[*] The reverse, however, seems to be true under nonthreat situations, where high-anxiety persons perform better than low-anxiety ones. An experiment was once undertaken involving a personal-threat situation in which college students were told that high school students with IQ's greater than 100 and most college students should be able to complete a particular task successfully, and a nonthreat situation in which students were told that the tasks were difficult and that they might not finish all of them—if they didn't finish them, they were not to worry about it. The nonthreat instructions seemed to reassure the high-anxiety persons, for they did better

Rod Laver, the wiry, red-headed "Rocket," is the greatest left-hander in history. His game is built around astonishingly quick reflexes and a bold and imaginative use of the wrist. The Aussie superstar is the only two-time winner of the Grand Slam.

[*] I. G. Sarason, "The Effects of Anxiety and Threat on the Solution of a Difficult Task," *Journal of Abnormal Social Psychology*, Vol. 62, pp. 165–68.

than the low-anxiety students. A person of high anxiety seems to be able to perform best when he is not in a threatening situation. A tennis tournament is similar to the personal-threat situation in the experiment, and the high-anxiety person is more likely to perform less well than a low-anxiety person. The experiment also showed that many low-anxiety persons perform better when they are told explicitly and emphatically that their level of performance on a task will reflect their intelligence level. This would suggest that tennis players of low anxiety will do best when spurred by a threat of some sort—or, of course, by an incentive, such as a sum of money, a prestigious trophy, or a college scholarship.

It is common knowledge that among athletes of equal ability some do well in competition, others don't. Of two shot-putters who both, day in and day out, make practice puts of, say, forty-four feet, one will put the shot forty-nine feet in competition, the other no more than forty-two. And in tennis, of two players who match each other game for game and set for set in practice, one will consistently beat the other in tournament play. The difference is in part, and possibly in large part, due to anxiety. The superior competitor controls his anxiety. It is comparatively rare that he suffers overanxiety and tries too hard and loses his timing and coordination. The inferior competitor cannot prevent anxiety from dissipating his abilities, which may be considerable, and enfeebling his efforts. However, at least one study of athletic ability has pointed out that able athletes victimized by overanxiety are likely to, in time, do well in competition.*

*Francis J. Ryan's "Investigation of Personality Differences Associated with Competitive Ability, and Further Observations on Competitive Ability in Athletics," *Psychosocial Problems of College Men*, Bryant M. Wedge (ed.), New Haven: Yale University Press, 1958, pp. 113–29. The author is indebted to Ryan's findings for this entire paragraph.

What are the kinds of things that will raise the average player's anxiety to a point where it is likely to interfere with his performance? The hierarchy of anxiety-provoking situations that follows lists the stimuli or situations in descending order according to the degree of anxiety they evoke. This hierarchy is based on my own experience and that of a number of other tournament players:

1. Final point of a tie breaker in the final set of the match.
2. Starting to serve at the beginning of the match.
3. It is the first set. You are the receiver and the score is 6–5, advantage out (for the fifth time).
4. It is the first set. You are serving and the score is 6–5, advantage in. While you are at the net, your opponent executes a driving lob which you are unable to get, but the ball bounces one inch beyond the baseline.
5. One hour before the match.
6. The night before the tournament.
7. One day before the tournament.
8. Two days before the tournament.
9. Three days before the tournament.
10. Four days before the tournament.

Not all tennis players would arrange the items of this hierarchy in the same order. Some might find the situation of starting to serve (Item 2) much less provocative of anxiety than the night before the tournament (Item 6). Needless to say, what you know, or what you think you know, about the playing ability of your opponent will affect your anxiety. Your opponent may scare you into believing that he is far better than you and that you do not have a chance to beat him. On the other hand, if a person who is good at evaluating tennis players tells you that you should beat your opponent 6–1, 6–1, then that assurance may well decrease your anxiety.

Sometimes the attempt of a noncompeting person to control the competitors' perceptions of a match can backfire. For example, Pancho Gonzales tried psychological warfare against the Australians during 1960 Davis Cup play. Sirola and Pietrangeli, the Italians, had won the right to play the Australians in the finals. Pancho volunteered to help the Italian team. Before the matches he made himself available to newspaper and television reporters. He predicted a victory for Italy. He said that Pietrangeli and Sirola were in a fine frame of mind and were as fit as they could be. He said, "I think they can win it," and added that Australia's Rod Laver appeared well below form and that the Australian number-one player, Wimbledon champion Neale Fraser, had reached his training peak and was on the verge of going stale. "They better not play Neale much tomorrow," he said, "or he will be off edge." As things turned out, his remarks spurred the Australians to intense practice and lulled the Italians into complacency. Laver and Fraser, under the whip of team captain Harry Hopman, were intense and grim as they practiced with professionals Lew Hoad and Ken Rosewall. The Italians, however, were carefree. Both Pietrangeli and Sirola clowned through their practice. The Australians had little difficulty trimming the Italians.

The closer in ability two tennis players are, the greater the likelihood of anxiety. If you have played your opponent several times in the past and each time the score was close, your anxiety is likely to be high the next time you play him. On the other hand, if your opponent is either much better than you or much worse, your anxiety is likely to be minimal. If before the match you perceive that it will be quite close, then you are likely to have much more anxiety than if you feel that you will defeat your opponent easily or that you are obviously no match for him.

In a close match the level of jitters will vary, going up at each crucial point in the match, such as at set or match point. In a game the crucial points are normally the third and the fifth; in a set the crucial games are the fourth, the seventh, and the ninth; in a three-set match the crucial set is the first; in a five-set match the crucial set is the third. To players prone to overanxiety, these crucial points, games, and sets can be traumatic. They seem to activate all that is self-defeating. Such a player, for example, will try to play it safe. He will become tentative in his play and, in effect, will give up on winning. He has lost his courage and is no longer able to meet crucial points without fear. Unlike him, a champion is never paralyzed by jitters at crucial points in a match. He is not afraid of the big point; he is mentally and emotionally up for it.

Laver is such a champion. In the course of his Grand Slam in 1962, Marty Mulligan had him match point, and Laver won. In his 1969 Grand Slam there were many crucial points, games, and sets. In a match with Dick Crealy, Crealy took the first two sets, and Laver won. Prejit Lall won the first two sets at Wimbledon; Laver came back and won. And he won the longest and hardest match of the slam—the one against Tony Roche in the semifinals of the National Singles Championships of Australia—7–5, 22–20, 9–11, 1–6, 6–3.

Confidence is proportionate to success. It will deteriorate in the face of continued failure; it will increase with each victory. Nevertheless, rigorous training according to a preset schedule can do much to promote it. But if you establish a schedule of training from, say, eight o'clock to twelve every morning, you can't skip a workout to go on a fun or a business trip. If you

Hard-hitting Australian player Frank Sedgman has won numerous singles championships including the United States, Wimbledon, Australia, and Italy. He could sprint one hundred yards in 9.9 seconds, and ran down practically any shot his opponent would hit. Gonzales felt that Sedgman was physically one of the strongest players he ever faced. With long hours of training he has always maintained himself in optimum physical shape.

Tony Roche's most outstanding quality is determination. Despite several operations on his playing arm, the Australian left-hander attacks relentlessly and has great retrieving ability. The tougher the game gets, the more Tony drives himself. He has a rich repertory of shots and is able to make them under pressure. His concentration is unsurpassed.

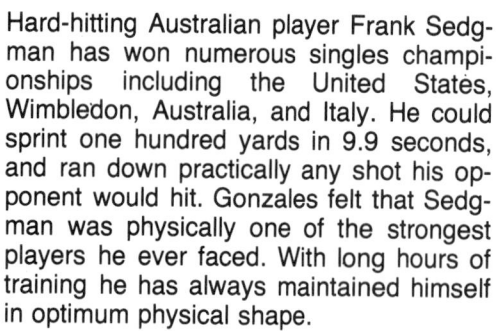

are plagued by the fear of a weak serve or backhand, you can eliminate this fear through training. Confidence and fear cannot exist at the same time; if you are to excel, you must dominate and control your emotions. Jitters will undermine your strokes by interfering with the proper movement of your muscles. They will make you hit the ball wide or long. They will impair your judgment. And they will cause you to shrink from the ball as you hit it. While confidence is not a guarantee of success in tennis, if coupled with skill it will go a long way toward making you a winner.

The preceding observations on anxiety leave us with this question: How can anxiety be controlled? The answer is the concern of the next chapter.

Chapter 5

Twenty-four Ways to Control Anxiety and Thus Boost Confidence

Even the best of players experience anxiety before a match. In 1976, Roscoe Tanner, after defeating Raul Ramirez and thereby leading the United States team to victory in the North American Zone Davis Cup competition, remarked, "I was more nervous today, and sleeping less well before the match, than at any semifinals at Forest Hills or Wimbledon." In his case, anxiety may have enhanced his performance. In general, however, great anxiety tends to worsen a player's performance by interfering with the body's ability to respond to the instructions of the mind. Also, it is unpleasant. Top players usually lose, or manage to control, their anxiety as a match progresses; second-rate players are victimized by theirs.

The twenty-four items of advice in this chapter can do much to enable the developing player to control anxiety, tension, and nerves and thereby heighten his confidence and his performance. But they must be approached sensibly. Since no one is quite like anyone else, everyone who wishes to get the most out of the following suggestions must adapt them to his or her distinctive makeup. Some experimentation will be necessary, and certainly a great deal of effort and persistence. To govern one's feelings is never easy, but efforts directed to that end always bring with them great benefits.

Before the Match

1. Remember that your opponent suffers from anxiety.

Competition, except the most inconsequential, provokes anxiety, for something—money, fame, prestige, pride, self-satisfaction—is at stake. Consider your opponent and ask yourself, "What does he or she have at stake in our match? You can always, if you use your imagination, supply an answer. And as soon as you apprehend

Roscoe Tanner has a lethal left arm which is said to guide a deadly serve at speeds up to 140 mph. A determined competitor who has worked hard to improve his game, he not only hates to lose, but can't stand himself when he does. When he falls behind in a match he only gets tougher.

what it is that matters to your opponent, you cut through the superficialities that so often impair one's play: an opponent's demeanor, which may be a mere mask of casualness or confidence; his past successes, which matter nothing to the challenge he now faces; and even his talents, which are in the service of what he wants now and are therefore, in a sense, different from the talents that served what he sought in the past. Once you have grasped the fact of your opponent's anxiety, you have found a weakness.

2. Enlist your anxiety in your behalf.

A child who is learning to walk totters, stumbles, falls, and gets hurt. Before his next attempt, and before succeeding ones, he is anxious. It is natural that he should be anxious; also it is natural that he should continue his attempts and that each attempt reduces his anxiety until eventually he learns to walk. One difference between a child struggling to walk and an adult struggling to be a first-rate tennis player is that the adult must advance himself consciously. He must concede to himself that he is anxious in the face of competition, that it is natural to be so, and that, moreover, it is natural to go ahead anyway and play for all he is worth. The result of such consciousness is, at the least, to control anxiety and, at best, convert it into a powerful ally. What is more, the benefits of control are not only mental but physical, for raw anxiety prepares the body to face stress, and controlled anxiety to overcome it. This, perhaps, explains why Chris Evert, before a match, gets away from people and "waits for the nervous feeling to come." She, like other winning players, knows how to take something as unpleasant as anxiety and turn it to her benefit.

3. Keep your match within a realistic perspective.

Things have a way of turning out well when they are kept within their proper place in one's life, and a way of turning out badly when they are inflated and elevated to the status of idols. Most idols are false idols, and false idols invariably bedevil idolaters, and sometimes crush them. This book assumes that tennis is a prominent, and maybe even an important, part of your life. And therefore, for the sake of good tennis, the advice is to recall that the Biblical declaration, "This too shall pass away," applies as much to the most dismal straight-set defeat on a local court as it does to victory at Wimbledon.

4. Develop anxiety tolerance through competition.

It is a common experience among tennis players that the second match of a day is preceded by less worry and nervousness than the first, the third less than the second. An acquaintance of mine who recently won a city tournament that necessitated his playing four matches in one day told me that he felt "loose as a goose" when the fourth match was about to start. An increasing tolerance of anxiety is an experience that is not confined to the successive matches of a day. By seizing every opportunity to engage in match play, a tennis player will soon find that the ability to suppress jitters is one of the permanent and ever-developing strengths of his game. His mastery of his nerves will never be absolute, but he will eventually discover that his self-control is adequate to enhance his abilities and heighten his fun.

5. Practice so that effective stroking becomes a reflex action.

The player who can serve, lob, smash, and hit passing shots well in practice play or in casual matches may discover that his game goes to pieces in tournament play. The pressures of serious competition can damage eye-muscle coordination. They can so impair the ability to judge distance that a player may be continually startled and perplexed as his shots fall long, go wide, or fail to go over the net. And they can so impede the contractions and extensions of leg and arm muscles that he feels drained of strength, speed, and agility. Such pressures are a form of anxiety or of a breakdown of confidence. They must be dealt with beforehand, and the proper way to deal with them is to make the physical elements of one's game, especially the strokes, so natural, so habitual, so reflexive that they are, in effect, set apart from the mental and emotional elements. The player who wants to attain a maximum degree of physical ease must not merely learn his strokes, he must overlearn them; that is, when he achieves what he supposes is mastery, he must strive for perfection, the pursuit of which makes possible genuine mastery—and well-founded self-confidence.

6. Realize that time reduces tension.

Tension, as most of us experience it, often seems to increase with the passage of time: we feel more and more unsettled in our stomachs; headaches intensify; constrictions in our chests make us feel caught in a tightening grip. The wrong response to tension is to give in to the feeling that our discomforts will continue and forget the fact that they will end. The right response is to dispel tension by seeing it as involved in time, and therefore not lasting. You may right now prepare yourself to exercise the kind of consciousness that banishes tension simply by recollecting how often you have endured and passed beyond it. And if you feel "tight" before a match, think of your tightness as about to pass and you will begin to loosen up.

7. Talk out tension.

Language is one of our most powerful means of controlling reality. In the case of our inner reality of feelings and emotions, language enables us to transform subjective states into objects. When we say "I am nervous" or "I am anxious" or "I am uneasy," nervousness, anxiety, or uneasiness is no longer a condition that we must passively endure or passively suffer. We have put it into words, and so made it a thing. We have *ex-pressed* it, which is to say, *pressed it out of us.* In a very real sense, we have put distance between it and us. Hence, the advice to talk out tension is in keeping with our natures, with the way we are made up.

When we express, or talk out, our feelings to someone in sympathy with us, not only do we detach ourselves from what has seized, occupied, and controlled our spirits but we also ask the person listening to us to assume and absorb it and carry it away. The more sympathetic our listener, the more he or she relieves us of our burdens.

The competitor who wishes to follow the advice to talk out tension must first recognize that to ease one's inner state through speech is perfectly fitting and proper to our natures. He must then intelligently and carefully decide to whom he will turn. Will it be his wife, or in the case of a woman, her husband? A parent? A friend? A fellow player? A coach or trainer? What matters is not the designation (friendship, marriage, and so on) of the relationship but rather the qualities of the person whom we will ask to aid us. The person must be worthy of trust and capable of sympathy. He should be someone who knows tennis—ideally, a player who is himself competitive and therefore familiar with the tension and anxiety we experience. He should be someone who knows that no matter how much you or the local newspaper or your fellow players may inflate the importance of your match, no tennis match shakes the world. He should be someone who is as reassuring as he is realistic. If he is one to say "This will be a hard match and you are in for a rough time" he should also be one to say "Why worry? You're going to give a good account of yourself, and you *can* win." Ideally, he should be someone whose calmness, sense of perspective, and inner poise are such that we can exchange our tension for his composure.

8. Jog.

We have all observed that, when tense or nervous, people naturally tend to be physically active: they pace about a room, they drum on a table with their fingers, they rapidly oscillate a foot. Such physical motion relieves tension. Research has shown that jogging—which in relation to tension may be considered a more coordinated, thoroughgoing, and beneficial tension-easing activity than pacing the floor—does much to promote inner calm, especially when accompanied by pleasant thoughts conducive to mental and emotional harmony. It is most advisable, then, to go out into the most pleasant surroundings you can find, jog until you feel properly exercised. While jogging think of get-togethers with your friends, happy family activities, such wholesome pursuits as boating or sight-seeing, or whatever else makes you feel good.

9. Engage in play and hobbies.

Play is an excellent way to relieve anxiety. Its great virtue is that it gives us a break from what is serious, demanding, and mentally taxing. Just as good farmers must allow portions of their land to lie fallow so that the soil's capacity for crop production may be renewed, so also those, such as tennis players, who subject themselves to stress must resort to ways whereby they may replenish their capacity to engage in stressful activities. Fun and laughter do just that. Adults must understand that play, despite its association with the things of childhood, is necessary at every stage of life. Serious tennis players should accept the fact that competitive tennis is *not* play, and they should therefore make an effort to schedule periods of play into their lives.

Likewise, hobbies—reading, music, gardening, whatever—serve to divert us from more serious pursuits, keep us from growing stale, and thereby enable us to return to our important endeavors refreshed and renewed. Like much of the advice in this book, the suggestion to engage in play and hobbies presupposes that we are many-sided beings and that our lives as entities must be sound if our particular, special pursuits are to be properly carried out.

10. Practice before your match.

I have noticed that Harry Hopman, preparing his team for Davis Cup matches at Forest Hills, would have his players practice serving for about half an hour before a match. To arrive at a match at least half an hour early and practice strokes (perhaps against a backboard) and serves (preferably to a player) enables you to dispel tension and anxiety while priming yourself for the match. You might also, after a warmup of about fifteen minutes, play a two-out-of-three mini-match with whoever is available. To forgo such prematch practice can seriously undermine one's game. I recently spoke with a junior player right after he had lost a match 6–4, 6–2. When I asked him why he had been so slow in getting his game together that he quickly fell behind 4–1 in the first set, he remarked that he had felt tense and tight at the start of play and added that his opponent had played a set with somebody else a while before their match. Get in a sensible amount of prematch practice.

11. Preplay a tough match in your imagination.

Many difficult experiences are less unsettling the second time we encounter them. To the extent that you can so visualize an upcoming match that you feel you are already in it, the actual match will seem like a rematch. Projecting yourself through imagination into a match is easier if you know your opponent. If you don't know him, you can still allow your imagination to work on what is available: the physical setting of the match, the time of day, the size of the crowd (inasmuch as you can estimate it), the degree of importance you attach to the match, your feelings. And so, when actual play is about to start, whatever may tend to heighten your anxiety will be reduced in potency by the feeling that you've already faced up to it.

12. Start early and use a checklist to get ready for a match.

We often tell ourselves to make a mental note to do something—and we often misplace our mental note. Notes are to be made in note pads. Since the preparation for a match involves getting together a number of articles of clothing, perhaps several pieces of equipment, water containers, and other things, it is wise to have a checklist of things to be gathered up and things to do and to have all items checked off well before you start for the court. A feeling of preparedness, and of your ability to do things systematically, is one of the small but real components of confidence.

13. Do what you can to change conditions conducive to anxiety.

It is part of life as many of us live it today to be in proximity to people and goings-on that disturb us. Frequently we must be resigned to this, for we cannot change the world to suit us. There are, however, occasions—such as the hours or even days preceding a tennis tournament of importance to us—when we must shake off our acceptance of things as they are and act decisively in our own behalf. If those around you make it impossible for you to maintain your composure, speak to them. If your surroundings are unsettling, remove yourself from them. When a tennis match represents an extraordinary occasion, challenge, or opportunity, be ready to resort to extraordinary means in order to get yourself into tip-top mental and emotional condition.

14. Use relaxation tapes or recordings.

Relaxation tapes and recordings are mechanical aids to tranquility and calmness. Since many of us rarely, if ever, make use of them, we may forget, or not even know, that they exist. Well, they do, and a librarian or a psychologist should be able to help you find one.

15. Relax your muscles and you alleviate tension.

It is because the mind and the body are in union that mental and physical tension accompany each other. All of us have been in situations—school examinations, business challenges, moments of consequence to our personal lives—where mental and emotional stress manifested themselves in muscular aches and constrictions. When the situations passed, so did our physical tension. Likewise, it is possible to reduce physical tension and thereby dispel mental and emotional unease. In fact, the trainers of many different kinds of athletes have long resorted to methods to get at the mental through the physical. Consider getting in touch with a physical therapist—preferably one who plays tennis—and have him decide on the right muscle-relaxing methods for you.

If you feel that relaxation does not require recourse to others, use your imagination to help yourself. Taking a hot bath can do much to relax the muscles and decrease tension. (However, using this method in the hours before a match can backfire. Enervation, or excessive relaxation, may result, and it may be impossible to get toned up by the time play commences. Hence, it is desirable to experiment with relaxation measures when no important match is imminent.)

16. Ten tricks to get to sleep.

1. Take a long walk.
2. Take it easy for the hour preceding bedtime. Intense mental activity, which is often conducive to wakefulness, should be avoided. Light reading or the watching of a pleasant television show helps many to get to sleep.
3. Drink a little warm milk if it agrees with you. Avoid barbiturates and liquor, which interfere with dreaming (an essential part of restorative sleep), promote irritability, leaves us with hangovers.
4. Take a warm bath.
5. See to it that your bedroom is free of drafts and moderately cool. Rooms that are too cold or too hot are bad for good sleeping.
6. Wear loose-fitting, comfortable night clothes.
7. Sleep only on a comfortable bed with a firm, even mattress.
8. Have your bedroom dark and quiet.
9. If it works for you, try counting backward from one hundred: "One hundred, relax, ninety-nine, relax..." and so on. If you are lying in a comfortable position, and your eyes are closed, you may be out before you reach eighty.
10. Put your body to sleep part by part. Starting with your toes and working upward, consciously relax each part of you.

If you should find yourself unable to sleep, avoid the moonlight madness of fretting over your wakefulness. Remember, most of us don't need half as much sleep as we think we do—what we need is rest, and we can get that without sleeping if we take it easy.

Though he is just a little guy, "Flying Dutchman" Tom Okker is one of the fastest men on the courts. He relies on his speed to "pick off" an opponent's shot; he is discreetly aggressive and has excellent confidence and ball control, plus a strong determination to win.

During the match

17. Take your time in serving.

Before serving, Jimmy Connors bounces the ball four times, straightens out his shirt (although it doesn't need adjusting), and taps the bottom of his shoes (even when there can't possibly be anything lodged in the soles). I have seen him take twenty-eight seconds between the completion of play for a point and his next serve. Torben Ulrich slowly positions his left foot close to the service line and then gradually moves the toe of his shoe ever closer to the line. Not only does he give the umpire the impression that a foot fault is unlikely but also he gives himself time to relax. Though players differ in the pace at which they approach the base line, those who take their time are less likely to serve badly as a result of hurry than those who rush. Establish the preservice ritual that is right for you and be in no hurry to go through it.

18. Take your time when getting set to receive serve.

When Tom Okker wishes to delay his opponent's serve, he attends to his racket and goes through the motions of adjusting the strings. When he feels prepared to receive serve, he looks up. Other players effect a delay in other ways. You can do much to keep yourself relaxed by establishing your way to control the pace of play, particularly before a second serve. If it is a matter of courtesy not to delay the game unduly, it is also a matter of reasonable self-interest to delay it long enough for you to feel right. And the Official Tennis Rule is on your side: if your opponent serves when you are not prepared to receive, he may not claim a point.

19. Relax legs, shoulders, neck muscles, and hands.

Between points, flexing and extending the legs, rotating the head, rotating the shoulders, and moving the fingers will help to keep you loose and distract you from any nervousness from which you may be suffering.

20. Breathe deeply during changeovers.

Conscious deep breathing with attention to the air passing through your nose and filling your lungs will, like the relaxation technique described in the preceding item of advice, distract you from your feelings and incline you to be more aware of your physical state. The attention you put into this activity will also make it easier to collect your powers of concentration when play is about to resume.

21. Affix yourself to the ball.

Keep yourself so intent on the ball that it seems to be a part of you, even when it is on your opponent's side of the court. An opponent may be a source of anxiety; a small sphere should not be.

22. Approach a match with aggressive determination.

Aggression and determination are incompatible with timidity and anxiety. We can't maintain both pairs of feelings at once and equally. Keep your mind focused on victory and on what you will to do achieve it; you will feel yourself aggressively and determinedly approaching your match. What is more, when you shake hands with your opponent, you will transmit your emotional strength, an awareness that will do nothing for his self-confidence.

23. During a match, do everything one step at a time.

In the midst of play, the thought of victory and all that must be gone through to attain it can overwhelm us.

Torben Ulrich of Denmark cuts an unusual figure on the courts. Though in his forties, he is fitter than most of the younger players. It is said that he runs fifteen miles daily and has rock-hard muscles. This shrewd, beloved mystic has fabulous endurance, unwavering concentration, and solid self-confidence.

Intense competition rarely allows for the mental perspective needed to take in properly the whole enterprise before us. Rather it inclines us to attend to one particular activity and then another. So when, for example, you are preparing to serve, you can effectually preclude the double-fault mania—a common destroyer of good play—by attending to, first, your preserve ritual, then the toss, then the stroke. As William W. Quillian, who was ranked tenth nationally a number of years ago, remarked, "If you get the first serve in, you won't double-fault; and if you ace your opponent, you won't doublefault." The thing to do, then, is to take care of step one before you direct your attention to step two.

24. Try the "shock approach."

When psychotherapists use the phrase "shock technique," they are referring to the practice of telling patients the opposite of what they expect to hear. Thus, instead of telling a nervous patient to calm down and relax, they tell him to get more nervous, get as nervous as possible. Such peculiar advice often leads to a peculiar result: a reduction of nervous tension. An anxious tennis player who adapts this technique to his own purpose may find the results as happy as the technique is odd.

Chapter 6

Psychological Preparation for Tournament Tennis

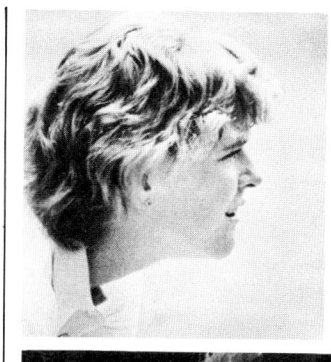

Traditional preparation for competition in tennis seems to be carried out in two main areas: (1) physical preparation, aimed at developing strength, endurance, flexibility, and so on, and (2) technical preparation directed at the mastery of tennis strokes. But a third area is becoming ever more important: the psychological preparation of the tennis player, including the study of tactics and the cultivation of the instinct to win. No longer is it believed that tennis deals only with the growth and development of strength, endurance, and suppleness. Today success in tennis, as in any other sport, requires the mobilization of all the player's physiological and psychological forces. The development of determination, concentration, judgment, planning ability, a readiness to react quickly to sudden and unexpected stimuli, the ability to tolerate frustration, and emotional control under stress have until recently been recognized only in an elementary way, with no assistance from a trainer. For this reason, many tennis players, well prepared in physical and technical respects, have failed to play up to their potential in competition, simply because they were not able to make maximum use of psychological factors.

At an NCNB Open Tournament in Charlotte, North Carolina, a few years back, I spoke with a number of prominent players about the matter of psychological preparation for a match. Charlie Pasarell said, "I'll visualize in my mind what I'll do. In games like basketball, teams learn about their opponent's plays, and then set up plays to counter them. In tennis it is different. About a half hour before a match, I find myself a secluded spot and start concentrating on how I'm going to play my man. There are a number of things that I think about. First, how to play this man, how to serve, and how he'll return the shots. During this period I think about the style of my opponent's game. I usually

Britain's Sue Barker has always been a keen competitor. Her father, a golfer, instilled competitiveness in her during her early years. He told Sue, "If you're four up, get five up," and she hasn't forgotten. She was the youngest in her family and had to fight her way up. Her outstanding tennis quality is determination; her concentration on tennis dominates her life.

know something about this from playing him previously. I visualize certain plays which will arise on the court, and I try to figure out how to handle them. I try to increase my degree of concentration. I also tell myself to control myself. At times I'm quick-tempered, and if I get a bad call, I might decrease my emotional control. So, I tell myself that I must be prepared for two or three bad calls, tell myself to keep cool and fight back. Besides, my opponent will get his share of bad calls. It is not easy to do all this. You have to practice this concentration just as you practice your strokes. It is difficult to just sit down and force yourself to do a good job of concentrating unless you have practiced it. I learned how to do this mental practice from Pancho Gonzales."

What Pasarell may have been doing besides preparing himself mentally is reducing his anxiety through the creation of imaginary scenes. This technique may not work for all tennis players because many people cannot imaginatively project themselves into playing situations involving a particular opponent—they just cannot form the visual images. Or, if images can be formed, they may not embody the reality that they do for Pasarell. It is reported that Pasarell still gets anx-

A true sportsman, Stan Smith has proved himself to be a strong competitor under the greatest pressure. Big and strong, he has a bludgeoning attack and a mighty first serve. He learned much about the game from Pancho Segura in Segura's Saturday morning clinic at the Pasadena Tennis Club. Through long hours of hard work and practice, Stan has achieved an excellent blend of concentration and self-confidence.

ious, as most players do, when he plays a close competitor, like Bob Lutz or Stan Smith, but his mental-practice technique has undoubtedly reduced this condition. Certainly it is in keeping with the theory and practice of such prominent psychiatrists as Dr. Joseph Wolpe, a professor of psychiatry at the Temple University School of Medicine and the Eastern Pennsylvania Psychiatric Institute and the author of *The Practice of Behavior Therapy*. Dr. Wolpe has successfully used a technique of "scene presentation" to alleviate anxiety. According to his theory, by anticipating an anxiety-provoking situation, and repeatedly imagining it, you reduce your anxiety.

Stan Smith, who has a fine playing temperament and is a cool competitor, prepares himself psychologically for his important matches days in advance. He said that psychological preparation begins as soon as he learns that he is accepted in a particular tournament, like Wimbledon. "All of your activities in one way or another are related to the match. Your sleeping, eating, social, and other activities are geared to this event. There are certain things like staying out late that you might do before your acceptance in this tournament, but you've got to practice and train diligently for this event. Then you think of the person whom you'll meet in the first draw. For, example, I played Morris in the first of the NCNB Open Tournament. I knew that he had gone to the quarterfinals at Wimbledon so he was not going to be a pushover. Also, I think of other players who will be in this tournament, like Roche, Ashe, and Richey. You start thinking how you'll play them. You actually play them psychologically before the real match."

Marty Riessen, who in 1968 had the highest won–lost record (fifty-five wins and fourteen losses) among American men, feels that proper psychological preparation entails the reduction of worries: "In this way, more mental energy is available for the tournament and I'm motivated and keyed up for each match.... Also, eating the proper food is important; otherwise, in a match your stomach is likely to act up."

Before a match, Arthur Ashe seems to prefer to keep his mind off it and he tries to relax by reading a book, seeing a movie, or watching television. About a half hour before the finals of the Charlotte tournament, a number of the players, including the finalists, Ashe and Smith, were in the lounge. Ashe was watching a professional basketball game on television and was deeply absorbed in it. Smith left for the court. Some fifteen minutes later Ashe was still watching the basketball game. Bob Lutz, sitting next to him, said, "You'd better got out there, you're late." Hesitatingly, Ashe left. It is probably not advisable to be as unmindful of an imminent match as Ashe apparently was of his, but a player who finds the hours immediately before a match particularly unsettling should at least be aware that for some first-rate players a period of utter disregard of the forthcoming contest is just the thing needed to avoid an attack of nerves.

Other players in the Charlotte tournament commented on the problem of staleness, which often arises as one proceeds from tournament to tournament. One of the players indicated his way of coping with the problem: "I may avoid thinking about an upcoming tournament altogether, until I am told who my first opponent is going to be. When I know who I am up against, I have something specific to think about. If I know, or can learn about, how he plays and what his weakness is, I can let my mind go to work on how I'll play him. I consider whether I'll go with hard or with soft shots. I think about how I'll vary my pace of play. This situation of having a particular challenge to prepare for affects the way I feel before a match."

The psychological value of such mental focusing can be enhanced if a player can draw on something tangible—namely, notes or other written information on an opponent—to prompt his thoughts and mental pictures. The keeping of information on the opposition is now customary in all sports, certainly in all professional sports. In tennis the practice goes back at least as far as the 1920s when Rene Lacoste, who won the United States Men's Singles Championship in 1926 and 1927 and the Wimbledon Singles in 1928, let it be known that he kept an intelligence file on other players. The late Perry Jones of the Southern California Tennis Association kept one, too. And it is said that members of that association often do better than expected against opponents from other areas of the country and opponents from overseas because they have so much information on the strengths and weaknesses of the opposition. They seek to know what they are up against before they get on the court rather than discover it in the course of play, and they settle beforehand on strategies and tactics. During play they are thus free to concentrate on pounding away at their opponents' weaknesses.

Of course, it just may be that the chief value of such information is not that it discloses in advance the contest we will be engaged in—every match has surprises in store for us—but that it gives us the feeling that we can to a degree settle things beforehand or at least stack the deck in our favor. In fact, we can. This is why psychological preparation is so important and also why it should not be thought of as existing apart from the physical and technical components of training, practice, and match play or from the information-digesting work of the intelligence.

The powers of the imagination should be directed not only to forthcoming matches but also to more immediate concerns, especially practice sessions.

Perhaps the most illustrious example of how an imaginative approach to practice sessions can enhance one's game is provided by Bjorn Borg. Observers of Borg when he practices have reported that he talks as little as when he is in a match. In fact, he approaches a practice play as if it were match play, for he believes that such an approach enables him to make what he does in a workout a permanent part of the array of skills he will employ in a tournament. The record of his successes indicates the soundness of his belief. Although everyone will agree that it is desirable to practice hard, not everyone recognizes that imagination and a great deal of mental discipline are necessary to keep a workout going at a high pitch. Because nothing like victory or defeat in match play is at stake, the boredom of repeating a particular stroke over and over again or the tiredness that comes of efforts leading to no immediate reward tend to make a player engaged in practice go easy on himself even when he wants to expend himself fully. If you want to get the most out of a workout, you must emulate Borg. You must use your imagination so that if, for example, you are executing a hundred consecutive serves, every one of them is for match point at Wimbledon. To use your imagination in this way will not only intensify your workouts but also reduce the difference that normally exists between a player's psychological state when he is practicing and his psychological state when he is competing.

At this point it will serve our purpose if we consider what some of the best players in the world regard as the chief mental characteristics of tennis champions. I presented the following questionnaire-chart to Evonne Goolagong, Chris Evert, Billie Jean King, Stan Smith, Bjorn Borg, and Ilie Nastase when they participated in the Second World International Tennis Classic held a few years ago at the Sea Pines Racquet Club in Hilton Head.

Evonne Goolagong Cawley is a natural athlete and a popular player with enormous talent and an easy, charming personality. At times the Australian seems to have difficulty concentrating; she has "walkabouts" when she appears to be highly distracted. One of the most colorful players of the modern tennis age, her will to win is superb.

Mental Characteristics Of Tennis Champions

1. Strong determination (willpower, motivation to win) — 1 2 3 Average 4 5 6 — Low level of determination

2. Aggressive (fighting spirit) — 1 2 3 Average 4 5 6 — Low level of aggressiveness

3. Highly competitive (tournament player) — 1 2 3 Average 4 5 6 — Doesn't enjoy competition, prefers "social" tennis

4. Bold in approach, especially when behind; changes game — 1 2 3 Average 4 5 6 — Afraid to change when behind

5. Dominant, wants to lead — 1 2 3 Average 4 5 6 — Submissive, easily led

6. Ruthless, never gives an inch — 1 2 3 Average 4 5 6 — Gives in easily to persuasion, courteous person

7. Emotionally stable, controls emotions; cool, calm — 1 2 3 Average 4 5 6 — Excitable, hyperemotional, anxious

8. Industry (seeks additional work, energetic) — 1 2 3 Average 4 5 6 — Seldom works even when pressured, lazy

9. Initiative (actively creative) — 1 2 3 Average 4 5 6 — Seldom initiates and mostly conforms

10. Responsibility (readily takes on responsibility) — 1 2 3 Average 4 5 6 — Avoids responsibility

11. Relaxed on and off court — 1 2 3 Average 4 5 6 — Always tense and nervous on and off the court

12. Realistic and objective — 1 2 3 Average 4 5 6 — Idealistic, dreamer, sensitive

13. Confident, unshakable, poised — 1 2 3 Average 4 5 6 — Lacks confidence, insecure

14. Perfectionist — 1 2 3 Average 4 5 6 — Sloppy in approach to doing things

15. Perseveres, never gives up, endurance, ability to take physical and mental torture — 1 2 3 Average 4 5 6 — Gives up easily, cannot stand mental and physical demands

16. Bright, very intelligent — 1 2 3 Average 4 5 6 — Mentally dull, low mental capacity

17. Good judgment and common sense — 1 2 3 Average 4 5 6 — Poor judgment and common sense; takes unnecessary chances

18. High level of concentration — 1 2 3 Average 4 5 6 — Easily distractible

19. Good planning ability — 1 2 3 Average 4 5 6 — Disorganized and cannot plan well

All six gave a high rating to characteristic 3: highly competitive.

Five of these six players gave high ratings to characteristics 1, 2, 6, and 15: strong determination, aggressive, ruthless, perseveres.

Five of the six gave a high rating to characteristic 4: bold in approach especially when behind; changes game.

Four of the six gave a high rating to characteristic 5: dominant, wants to lead.

Four of the six gave a high rating to characteristic 18: high level of concentration.

When these ratings are collated, a profile of a tennis champion emerges: A champion is determined, aggressive, highly competitive, bold and adaptable, dominant, ruthless, perservering, and strong on concentration.

This profile will be more meaningful if we note what characteristics these six players did not, generally, give high ratings to: emotional stability, initiative, responsibility, tranquility ("relaxed on and off court"), realism and objectivity, perfectionism, intelligence, good judgment, good planning ability. It is not that these characteristics are unimportant; it is simply that the others were considered to be of somewhat greater consequence to success in championship play.

When the players were asked how the characteristics that they regarded as most important might be developed and nurtured early in life, they gave answers such as these:

"Have the youngster work for things."

"Encourage the child to try harder the next time he faces a task."

"Get the young player into as many tournaments as possible."

"Teach kids never to give up."

"Always encourage a young boy or girl to do his or her best in every situation."

Adults who wish to develop the psy-

Andrea Jaeger is an outstanding player and a potential major tournament winner. She was fourteen years old when she turned pro in 1979, and in 1980 she reached the last eight at Wimbledon, was runner-up to Chris Evert Lloyd in the U.S. clay court championships, and became the youngest semifinalist in the history of the U.S. Open. She has had straight set wins over Rosie Casals, Sue Barker, Barbara Jordan, Betsy Nagelsen, Renata Tomanova, Ivanna Madruga, Virginia Wade and Wendy Turnbull.

chological virtues of champions will not often be told by others to "work for things," "try harder," and "never give up." They must tell themselves. Moreover, they must understand certain things that are beyond the grasp of children and that even when understood may be extremely difficult to accept. Aristotle, speaking of moral virtue, by which he meant good habitual powers, implied that virtues—courage, moderation, good sense, and so on—are not separate things but aspects of one thing, virtue; and he implied that to possess one virtue is to possess all virtues (and to be missing one is to be missing all). We cannot here consider whether the great Greek philosopher was right or how most of us must judge ourselves if he was; but we can derive from his way of thinking about human nature a notion that may apply to the matter of psychological preparation for a tennis match: developing inner strength for one kind of activity should be thought of as inseparable from developing inner strength for all kinds of activities. It is probably a fantasy to suppose that a person can be purposeless and undisciplined in a number of important areas of life and yet be purposeful and disciplined in tennis. Realism, and a sense of the relatedness of things, requires us to understand that we can best strengthen our psyches for tennis matches if we strengthen them for our other concerns through the methods that have been presented here: to use our imaginations to anticipate what is upcoming and to attend to what is present; to acquire knowledge and information before they are needed; to face squarely worries and anxieties until their power over us is enfeebled; and, when necessary, to direct our minds completely away from the serious things that confront us.

Chapter 7

On Capturing Momentum in a Match

The notion of momentum, as applied to sports, is a borrowing from the physical sciences, where it denotes the force of motion. When people speak of momentum in an athletic contest, they are usually expressing their perception that things are going well for one team or one player in such a way that they are likely to go even better as play continues. The notion seems especially applicable to a sport like football, where the progress of a team from one side of the field to the other allows us to perceive momentum as a sort of horizontal gravitation: the advance of the ball is linear, and as the team in possession of the ball gets closer and closer to the goal line the advance is felt to be ever more rapid and irresistible; but if the ball is fumbled or intercepted, the team without momentum may suddenly be down by seven points. We can see from this a peculiarity of momentum in athletic contests in general. When momentum is in operation, it seems to reveal how a team or player is doing and what the final score is likely to be; but when all points and scores are tallied, it may sometimes be seen to have meant nothing. The developing tennis player should therefore keep in mind that it is his or her general proficiency and mental condition that give meaning to any attempt to capture momentum in a match.

While participating in the Pro-Am event of the 1976 Almaden Tennis Grand Masters held at the Seabrook Island Club in South Carolina, I spoke to a number of the notable players there to find out how momentum is embodied in a good player during a match. Vic Seixas said, "Momentum is the outward sign that you are playing so well that you are gaining ground. It is primarily a mental emotional thing often brought on by something that makes you feel in charge of the situation." Tom Brown, a three-time winner in Davis Cup matches and a two-time winner in

Wimbledon doubles, said, "When you have momentum, you are concentrating harder, playing harder, and applying more pressure than your opponent; you're resisting discouragement better than he is; and maybe you've gotten a break—the ball hit the net but went over, or there was a bounce on your opponent's side of the net." Torben Ulrich likened momentum to progressing from a walk to a run, "until, at a certain stage of the game, you are leaving your opponent behind and both of you sense that he can't keep up with you." Other players spoke of momentum as involving "a feeling of contentment with yourself that leads to better play," "a more positive attitude that follows a lucky break or the winning of a few points by some good hard shots," "an upsurge of aggression followed by free swinging."

From observing the performance of such successful players as these, and also others—Rod Laver, Clark Graebner, Raz Reid—one can specify both the external and the internal elements that create momentum. The external ones include these:

- a lucky break (a favorable bounce, a net shot that goes over)

Victor Seixas is a great natural athlete who began playing tennis at the age of six. Ranked in the Top Ten twelve times between 1948 and 1966, he was No. 1 in the United States in 1951, 1954, and 1957. Vic has an effortless, powerful, high-kicking serve which provides excellent cover for his constant advances to the net. He combines fast reflexes, keen anticipation, and a superb volleying touch with stamina and calm determination.

Peter Blair Fleming has shown a remarkable development of mental toughness in his career. In 1974 he ranked fortieth in U.S. singles; by 1979 he had improved his standing to eighth in the nation and sixth on the USTA's prize money board. Fleming and John McEnroe form the best doubles team in the world. In 1979 they won the Wimbledon, the U.S. Open, and the Masters.

Francoise Durr, from France, has been ranked among the top ten women champions in the world. Her tennis style is unorthodox—she hits her backhand with a forehand grip. A steady player with good concentration, she displays a strong fighting spirit and never gives up.

- the winning of a crucial point
- a period of play in which you win a series of points by smashes or hard hitting
- a period of play in which you find yourself able to swing more freely than you usually can
- a favorable line call
- an ace, or an unreturnable serve, at a crucial moment
- a period of play in which everything you hit falls either just where you want it to fall or just within bounds
- the passing away of an external distraction

What all of these elements have in common is that they involve something exceptional, or at least out of the ordinary. Two of them—a lucky break, a favorable decision by the referee—may be considered outside the control of a player. The rest of them are all, to a greater or lesser degree, linked to the internal elements that create or contribute to momentum. The comments and self-analyses of the players I've mentioned indicate that the internal elements include the following:

- the discovery of an exploitable weakness in your opponent
- an upsurge of energy, mental or physical or both
- concentration superior to your opponent's
- superior effort
- superior aggressiveness
- superior self-confidence
- the feeling that your timing and the other subtle components of your game are right
- the sense, shared by your opponent, that your application of pressure is enabling you to pull ahead
- a feeling of mental–physical looseness

Before addressing the question of how to capture momentum in a match, we should consider a preliminary question that you might, with good reason, ask: namely, considering the general complexity of a match and the great number of things a player will have on his mind before and during a match, is it worthwhile, or even possible, to pay special attention to the complex and subtle matter of momen-

Martina Navratilova is a powerful left-hander who defected to the United States from Czechoslovakia. She is blessed with natural talent and great physical strength. Her attacking style puts her in a class with Billie Jean King and Margaret Court. On the court, her manner is proud and self-assured.

tum? The answer is, in brief, yes. All of us have tremendous capacities for handling complexities and for doing a number of things both simultaneously and well. Part of the proof of this is that we are frequently unaware of the complexities involved in activities that we handle easily: we simply take them in stride. Most of us who drive cars feel that driving is a simple activity, and yet when on the road we are continually varying the pressure on the accelerator, shifting the wheel from left to right by a few degrees, looking ahead, glancing in the rear- and the side-view mirrors, holding in mind our destination and our route, reading signs, and so on—and often, moreover, doing all of these things while listening to the radio and talking to a passenger. At times we want to pass a slower-moving vehicle, and so we do a number of additional things.

Gaining momentum on the court can be likened to passing a car on the road: there is nothing especially mysterious or overwhelming about it; you simply have to know what you are doing. You have been taking the first step while reading this chapter, for in seeing momentum as the result of internal and external elements you have been removing it from the realm of mystery and seeing it in terms of what social psychologists call "field theory," the idea that at any given moment positive and negative forces are at work whose net result is one of three things: equilibrium (you and your opponent are playing equally well; the match is nip and tuck), positive momentum (you are pulling ahead), negative momentum (your opponent is pulling ahead). Field theory presupposes the possibility of analysis followed by action. Once this is understood and accepted, you are prepared to take the other steps toward capturing momentum in a match:

- If you are the beneficiary of a favorable call by the referee or a favorable bounce, let your mind seize on it as a good omen and thereby release your positive psychic juices.
- Conversely, if your opponent is the beneficiary, fight off the superstitious feeling that the gods

69

of the court have it in for you. It takes only an instant to recall that every player from Borg on down gets bad bounces and bad calls.

- Exercise the mental discipline to blot out from your mind the loss of a crucial point. To be obsessed with the losing of a point is to be obsessed with losing. If a phrase like "You can't win them all" strikes you as a dead cliché, devise a fresh phrase to express the same truth. What matters is that you find the words to realize the actuality that a lost point is only a point.
- On the other hand, when a point crucial to the outcome of the match is in the offing, force yourself to imagine it as the point that decides and ends the match. If you do this, and if your opponent does not, you have the edge in the mental side of the contest. If you and your opponent are of comparable physical and technical ability, you have the edge, period.
- Draw on all your abilities to dispel internal and external distractions so as to intensify concentration: the correlation between concentration and momentum is direct.
- Be especially attentive to finding a weakness in your opponent. When you find one, belabor it as a prizefighter does a cut over the other fighter's eye. You will be maximizing the potency of your offensive play, forcing your opponent to play defensively, and heightening the mental side of your game with the discovery that you have found a gap leading directly to victory.
- Since momentum may be conceived to be the breaking up of equilibrium, change your game whenever you sense that the positive and negative forces are starting to align themselves so as to retard your momentum or to produce a state of balance in which momentum is up for grabs. You might, for example, increase the angle of your volleys or increase the depth and speed of your serves or ground strokes.
- Prompt yourself mentally and emotionally by using words as talismans. In transcendental meditation, the uttering of a mantra leads to a state of invigorating relaxation; in competitive tennis, the repetition of a word or phrase like "better!" "harder!" "more now!"—or whatever one you settle on—leads to intimidating aggression.

Inasmuch as momentum is the result of a field or network of forces, the foregoing suggestions represent ways of transforming forces that operate on you into forces that you direct. Probably every respectable player intuitively carries out one or more of them. Your intention should be to consciously practice and master all of them. If it becomes second nature to put into effect whichever of them a game situation calls for, and to do so with sustained efficiency, you are likely to capture and maintain momentum against an opponent who is in most respects your equal but whose grasp of the mechanics of momentum is partial and uncertain.

Chapter 8

Know Your Opponent and Playing Conditions

"What enables the good general to strike and conquer, and achieve things beyond the reach of ordinary men, is foreknowledge." These words, from *On the Art of War,* by Sun Tzu, epitomize the thinking behind the "intelligence operations" of most team and many individual sports today. Football, baseball, basketball, and other teams, boxers and chess players, tennis players—amateur as well as professional—employ the equivalents of army reconnaissance units to go one up on their opponents, who are, of course, following suit. Inevitably, counterintelligence—sometimes in the form of security personnel—has arisen and established itself as an important part of a team's activities.

Whatever a fan may think of such doings and their effect on sports, the fact remains that the practice is by now firmly established, and not only teams but also individual competitors must take into account that a contest will, at least in part, turn on what lies between the covers of a notebook. Moreover, intelligence and foreknowledge often enable an athlete whose physical gifts are unexceptional to stand up well against, and often surpass, an opponent whose athletic abilities in the usual sense—size, strength, speed, coordination—are greater. What is more, the "heady" player is a delight to behold. Not only does he please by providing a contrast with the more physical player, but he also encourages and inspires athletes whose age or stature or other physical attributes may not make for success in athletic contests.

As international competition in tennis becomes even more prominent than it already is, it is likely that scouting and other forms of information gathering will become increasingly sophisticated and systematic. That such activities are not yet as emphasized in tennis as they are in other sports might well encourage the developing player to turn to them in the

Margaret Smith Court thoroughly enjoys tennis. She has amassed a staggering total of major world titles and has deserved confidence in her ability. Though she has an insatiable appetite for success, she has had problems handling match nerves, which have at times cost her an international title.

reasonable expectation that they will not be countered by similar measures on the part of opponents. Of course, most players will not have the time or means to do anything like what a well-financed team or professional athlete can do to "get the book" on the opposition, but they can nevertheless do a lot and do it well.

The primary objectives of information gathering are two: to reduce your uncertainty about an opponent and to enable you to settle on a game plan.

The first of these objectives is important to the mental toughness with which you want to enter a match. To the extent that an opponent is an "unknown quantity"—a question mark—your imagination can fill with all sorts of doubts, misgivings, and anxieties that can enfeeble your spirits and, in effect, handicap you for play. But inasmuch as you know, or know of, your opponent, you can tell yourself, "I know what I'm up against; he's a human being; he has his weaknesses, which I can exploit; he has his strengths, which I can avoid or cope with. Now, let's get down to business and figure out a plan." The second of these objectives—preparedness for deciding on a plan—is equally important to establishing a positive, optimistic frame of mind. To have a plan based on reliable information allows you to look ahead to the opening minutes of play as a period when you may well so unsettle and confuse your opponent that he may never manage to get his game or himself together. If your information and foreknowledge are really sound, you may even be able to anticipate just how your opponent will try to adjust to your tactics and you can thus prepare backup plans to counter his countermoves. At the least, such intelligence and planning operations are fun and help to make tennis a proper game for beings endowed with brains.

Pros do this sort of thing, and it works for them. Bobby Riggs, before his Battle of the Sexes match against Margaret Smith Court in 1973, scouted her and noted the strength of her serve, her volley, her overhead, and her forehand, and the weakness of her backhand and of her ability to handle soft shots. In the match, he avoided her forehand as much as possible, went after her backhand, and hit a lot of floaters, spin shots, and drop shots. Riggs won. Billie Jean King saw the match and scouted Riggs for his strengths and weaknesses. Later, she got more information on him from Dennis Van der Meer. In the second Battle of the Sexes match, King defeated Riggs.

Intelligence operations in tennis comprise three activities: the gathering of information, evaluation, and interpretation.

As for the first of the three, your sources of information will include your own observations of an opponent whom you may have played or watched in action against someone else; the observations of friends; the observations of those who have played him; and newspaper, magazine, and broadcast reports. Although your own observations will naturally count most with you, you should not discount the observations of others merely because you may have had the opportunity of direct observation. Objectivity requires that you at least view your own perceptions in the light of what others have perceived. As a rule, when gathering information, neglect nothing; do not disregard any source.

Evaluation of information is a determination of its credibility, accuracy, and relevance. To determine the credibility of information that has come your way from sources other than your own observation, you must pass judgment on your informant. Is he reliable? Does he have sufficient tennis experience and ability to know what to look for and to view or adjust his perceptions against the not so obvious factors in a match? An inexperienced observer might accurately report that a particular player looked slow in moving about the court. An experienced one might report the same, but would be likely to note the surface played on and perhaps other conditions and considerations that accounted for the observed player's slowness.

The value of playing experience in a reporter can be clearly seen in television coverage of sports. A professional broadcaster will report that a boxer, for instance, delivered "a devastating left hook"—everyone in front of a television set heard the loud *thump* of leather against flesh and accepts the broadcaster's comment as accurate—and then a former professional fighter, in the broadcast booth for "color" commentary, will observe, "Well, Howard, I think that left met with a lot of leather before it glanced off his chin." Or a broadcaster will note that a particular tennis player looks sluggish on the court against his opponent, and then Tony Trabert, or some other former pro now broadcast-

Tony Trabert began playing tennis at the age of six. Determined to become an outstanding tennis player, he was generally the first one on the court after school and the last one to leave. Tony has the all-around Big Game, and uses the Kramer-style strategy of serve and advance to the net. Behind the smiling face there lies tremendous determination, great confidence, and splendid concentration.

ing, will recall that in a previous match the player who now appears sluggish at first held back in order to pace himself and later took command and won the match.

If high-paid, attentive professional broadcasters can be notoriously mistaken in their observations on a contest, how reliable can an observer be who may be inexperienced in the sport he is watching and who is not being paid to provide complete and accurate information? The point is not that you should disregard what such an observer tells you but that you must exercise your imagination and assess your informant and so put a sensible valuation on the information he has offered.

When you have passed judgment on the credibility of a source, you must judge the accuracy of the information it yields. The two judgments are related to but distinct from each other, for a credible informant may offer inaccurate, mistaken, or misleading information—we are all fallible. Accuracy is largely a matter of corroboration and confirmation by means of other, related information. Separate items of information on the same matter are measured and checked against one another. You note points of agreement; you do your best to account for inconsistencies and contradicitons; and finally you allow a conviction to form: "I must expect more trouble from my opponent's forehand than from his backhand." Since your judgments on accuracy of data can be at best intelligent and systematic, never absolutely scientific and certain as mathematical deductions can be, your conviction will be a provisional or conditional one—in practical terms, what happens when you are on the court with your opponent will cause you to discard some of what you have learned about him, cling to some of it, and estimate anew the rest of it.

Interpreting your harvest of information about an opponent may be viewed as boiling it down to a list of strengths, weaknesses, and stylistic peculiarities; an estimate of the kind of game you will face; and a formulation of strategies and tactics. If you have information on many aspects of your opponent's game, your analysis will proceed in step-by-step fashion, taking one aspect at a time. Since, however, all of the components of his game will be encountered together, during your match, ultimately your systematic analysis must result in an imaginative synthesis; that is to say, you must at last stop thinking and figuring and sit back and *see* with your mind's eye the match you will be in. You should have a clear and vivid vision of the things you want and need in order to prepare for the contest. The more complete your information, the clearer your vision will be. The more concentrated and intent your mental effort, the more vivid it will be. But since no one ever plays quite as he has played before, you can be sure that what you envision is not exactly what you will experience. Even if your opponent's game in general is consistent with his previous games, the details will vary. Nevertheless, if you have done your homework, you should be able to retain your composure in the face of the unexpected, make whatever adjustments are necessary, and turn in a creditable performance.

It is desirable that you have a system for keeping in order the information you collect. You should keep, ideally in a file, a separate information sheet on each opponent. If you are likely to draw on a number of sources, you might have for each of your opponents separate sheets, each limited to the information provided by one source. The form of the information sheet is up to you, but in general you will record at the top the name of an opponent and beneath it the source of your data. One section should be limited to notations on the speed, accuracy, control, direction, depth, and so

Julie Heldman has been consistently in the United States Top Ten. In 1968 and 1969 she was ranked number two in the United States, and in 1969, fifth in the world. She has fast reflexes and superior footwork, and is never afraid to try something different in a match. She is known for her tremendous fighting spirit and excellent concentration. Her mother, Gladys Heldman, was editor and publisher of *World Tennis,* and her father, Julius Heldman, won numerous national tournaments.

on of his shots:
- serve
- backhand
- forehand
- lob
- smash
- other

Another section might be devoted to remarks on the basic divisions of his game:
- net game
- base line game
- service reception
- volleys
- cross-court play
- down-the-line play

A third section might deal with his physical capacities:
- speed in general
- age
- side-to-side mobility
- vertical mobility
- stamina

A fourth section might remark on the mental and emotional character of his game:
- ability to handle external distractions
- ability to handle internal distractions; composure under stress
- preferences in regard to
  indoor/outdoor play
  court surface
  time of day
  equipment (e.g., balls)
  crowds/privacy
  other

You might include near the bottom of your information sheet general, or summary, sections: opponent's overall strengths; opponent's overall weaknesses; kind of game opponent plays—and, of course, sections that pertain to how you will deal with him: basic strategy to employ, specific tactics, and so forth.

One anecdote that illustrates how an item of information can help turn failure into success: In a recent local tournament I went up against a Navy lieutenant about whom not much was known except that he played number one on an eastern university tennis team. He played the net about 80 percent of the time. He went to the net with every serve. His forehand was relatively weak and his backhand was unusually good. He beat me rather easily. I tried passing him with drives on the right and left sides, lobbing, chopping; but none of these efforts seemed to work. I did notice that he missed more shots on his forehand than he did on his backhand.

I talked to a local player who beat him by coming to the net as often as possible, and in this way reducing the number of times that the lieutenant came to the net. Using this information, I beat him the next time we played.

Besides obtaining information about your opponent, you should obtain information about the surroundings where you will play. First, what kind of court is it? If it is a clay or rubico court, you can expect that you and your opponent will recover many shots which you might not recover on courts with a different surface, like concrete.

A west-southwest wind of up to twenty-five knots an hour, with gusts, was a significant factor in Rod Laver's 6–4, 6–2 defeat of Stan Smith in a CBS Tennis Classic a few years back. It virtually deprived Smith of perhaps his most potent weapon, his serve, by interfering with his ball toss. Consequently, other parts of his game failed him. Laver, on the other hand, seemed to get sharper and more self-assured as Smith got sloppier and more frustrated. It seemed that he was at times able to capitalize on the wind. In the first set, for example, leading 5–2, Laver got into position to serve and then moved six feet to the left, giving the impression that the strong wind was forcing, almost blowing, him out of his normal serving position. Then he returned to the regular spot. Smith looked on, appearing amazed at all this, seemingly convinced he was playing in a gale.

Before the match, Smith practiced on a court next to the clubhouse, which blocked the wind, and most of his practice consisted of ground strokes and volleys, with only an occasional serve. As a result, he was hardly prepared for the conditions that prevailed on the court where he played Laver. Laver, who warmed up against me, used a court where he could serve in the wind, and so was prepared to cope with the wind during the match.

Wind can blow in three general directions: from behind you, at you, or cross-court. But it is seldom in a precise 90-degree or 180-degree direction in relation to where you are standing. At times it can shift directions rapidly, perhaps blowing in three or four different directions during the course

Ken Rosewall is known by his adoring fans as "Little Ken," "Little Master," or "Muscles." The quiet, self-disciplined Aussie plays the big game despite his small size. Through diligent training he has developed one of the greatest backhands in the game. He displays superb self-confidence and unrelenting concentration.

Cliff Drysdale, a native South African, now lives in Dallas, Texas. One of the few successful baseline players, he depends upon his extremely accurate, two-fisted backhand. He reaches his peak when opponents hit to his backhand and rush to the net, only to find themselves helplessly overwhelmed by accurate passing shots crosscourt or down the line. This deadly backhand has pulled him out of many tough spots and added to his strong confidence.

of a single game. A few more pointers:

First, a long follow-through on all strokes promotes direction control of the ball. When playing with the wind coming from behind you, there may be an advantage in taking the net, since your opponent's passing shot will travel at less than usual speed and you will have more time to reach the ball. When your opponent takes the net, go for the passing shot. Your opponent's lob is likely to be short when he hits into the wind, and you will be in a better position to put it away. Be very cautious when you lob. When playing against the wind, your balls will travel more slowly and the lobs are apt to fall closer to the net. When you lob, lob very deeply. If there is a crosswind, drive your shots toward the side from which the wind is coming so that the wind will carry them into the court. When serving on windy days, reduce the ball toss and compensate for the lower toss by speeding up your swing.

If the type of ball makes a big difference in the way you play, accustom yourself to all types and brands of balls. Before a tournament, check with officials to determine what brand of ball will be used; then practice with them.

Chapter 9

Psychological Warfare

A couple of years ago, the sponsors of a tennis tournament to be held in Houston placed an advertisement in a newspaper. The ad depicted a cowboy in full regalia—black hat, boots and spurs, holster and cartridge belt, leather gloves—and with his weapon at the ready. The weapon was a tennis racket. The ad read, "The top guns in tennis are headed for a showdown in Houston . . . and when the smoke clears on December 12th, there will be no lone star survivor standing at The Summit in Houston, Texas. . . . To see this exciting shootout, check with your Delta Airlines agent."

This ad says something, if not about the sport of tennis, then at least about changes that have altered the image of tennis, the place of tennis in our society, and, to an extent, the activities to be seen on as well as around tennis courts. Tennis will always be a proper sport for men who are gentlemen and women who are ladies. But inevitably the game will reflect the forces—and not all of them are good ones—current in our society and these forces will at times make it difficult, impossible, or even undesirable for a player to participate in tennis as it was played in the past, or in some idealized version of the past. The tennis-player-as-gunslinger advertisement indicates that the game is now being, as we say, "hyped"—supercharged with images and suggestions that operate on our minds (to say nothing of our checkbooks) to make us regard tennis as a means of touching life at its most intense and dramatic. Add money to the psychological brew, and matches—especially the televised ones between the best professionals—soon start to gather about themselves the aura and atmospheré of *The Iliad*. And the spear rattling or pistol toting that goes on often takes the form of psychological warfare or, what is akin to it, gamesmanship.

Because people are impressed and influenced by what they see on tele-

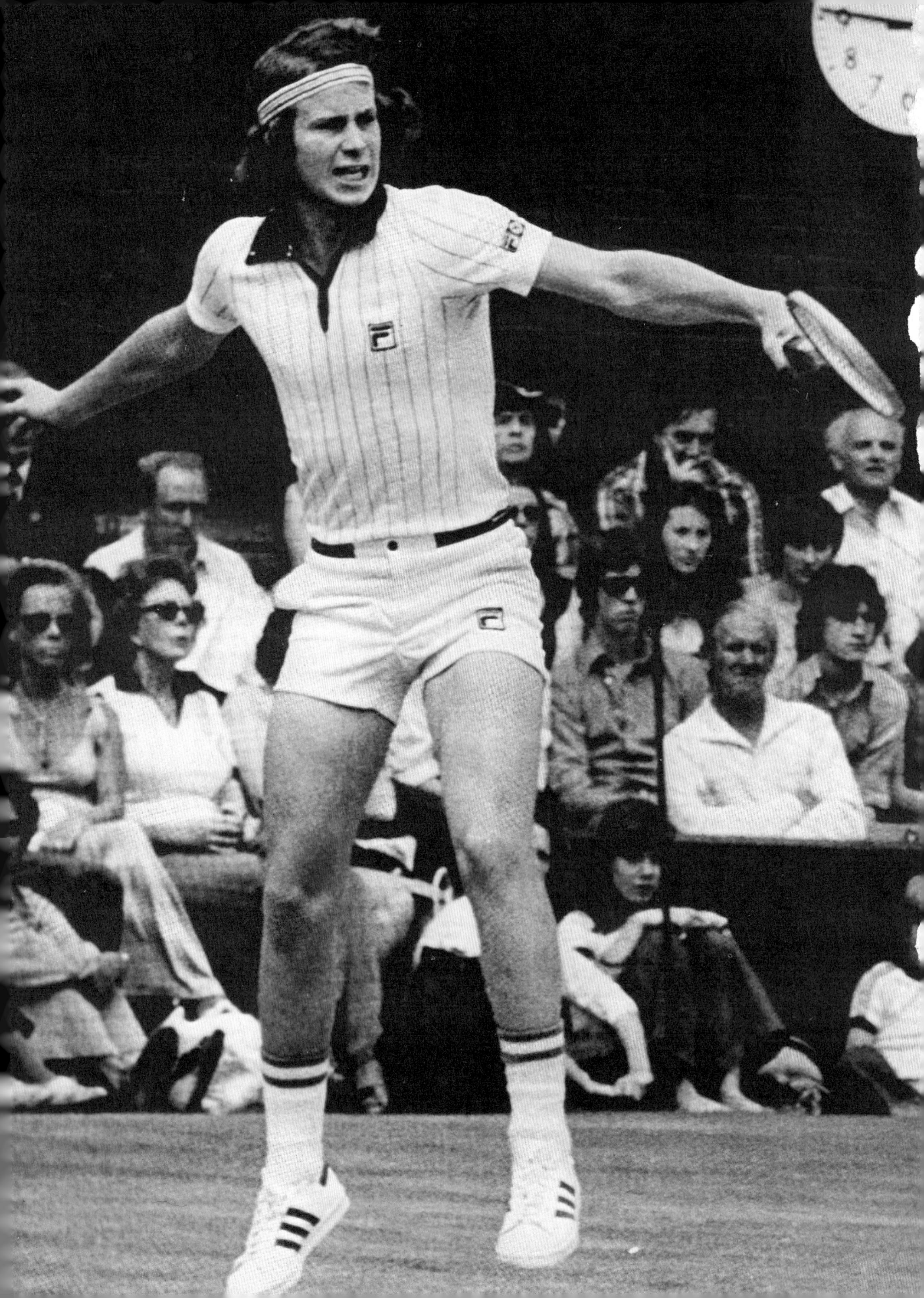

vision or read about in newspapers and magazines, the way professionals perform and behave filters down to the courts where amateurs play and shows up in one form or another. A McEnroe or a Borg, an Evert or an Austin, is duplicated thousands of times in the imitative mannerisms of amateurs. And a player's televised attempts to unsettle an opponent by methods that have nothing to do with playing skill will sooner or later, grossly or deftly, be copied and displayed in countless playgrounds and country clubs.

Every developing player, then, must at least be prepared for the psychological warfare and gamesmanship that may be used against him.

I once played in a tournament and encountered a particularly nasty kind of psychological warfare. The evening before my match a sponsoring organization had a party. One of the persons helping with the preparations

Tracy Austin grits her teeth with grim determination during her game with fellow Californian Diane Desfor, whom she defeated 6-1, 6-8, 6-4, in the first round of the Ladies Singles of the Wimbledon Championships in June 1978.

Left-hander John P. McEnroe Jr. is one of the youngest male players to rank in the nation's Top Ten. Ranked number ten at age 17 in 1977, he moved up to five in 1978 and one in 1979. He won the 1979 and 1980 singles championships at the U.S. Open, and in 1980 was a finalist at Wimbledon. In 1980 McEnroe and doubles partner Peter Fleming won the Wimbledon, the U.S. Open and the Masters.

became friendly with me, and I took to him warmly. We learned a little about each other. The next day, as my opponent and I were warming up shortly before the start of the match, my new friend passed by the court and said, "Walt, your wife just called you long-distance." He walked away too quickly for me to get more information about the call or to find out whether there was an emergency that had prompted it. I became quite unsettled and distracted, and play was to begin in a minute. Should I ignore the call for now? Should I interrupt the warm-up to return the call? I felt sure that my wife would not call me—but there *was* the possibility of an emergency. My opponent asked me whether I wanted to return the call. I said, "No," and, doing what I could to put the call out of my mind, played the match—which I lost. Afterward, I called my wife and learned that she had not called.

I later asked a number of players what they thought of this "psych job." Gardnar Mulloy said, "If someone tried to psych me as they tried to psych you, that would mean he was really afraid of me. I would leave the court and find that 'friend' and if I discovered it was a scheme, I would punch him in the nose." Fred Stolle, the Australian champion, said, "If anybody tried to psych me like that, I would figure out how to psych him in return." Jimmy Connors said, "That's not gamesmanship, that's being a [expletive deleted, though apt]. That should not be part of a game. I don't yet have a wife, but if someone said that my mother had called me, I know my mother well enough to know that she would not call me." Marty Riessen said, "I would not pay any attention to it."

Psychological warfare is the self-serving use of propaganda and other things to influence the opinions, emotions, attitudes, and behavior of hostile, neutral, or friendly groups. Psychological-warfare operations almost always rely on manipulative communication—taking the word "communication" in its widest sense. In athletics, gamesmanship is the art of winning by means of conduct that may or may not be in violation of rules but that invariably exploits them as fully as possible to unsettle, distract, or otherwise undo an opponent. In competitive sports, psychological warfare and gamesmanship frequently go together, and the two have become more and more conspicuous in tennis.

I once met with both in a match I played. My opponent played either on the base line or about one yard within it. I knew that my playing the ball deep was necessary to defeat him. Each time I hit the ball behind him but within the base line or close to the sideline, instead of indicating by hand that my shot was good, he would go to the spot where the ball had hit and stare down at it as if in doubt whether the ball had been in. This conduct was distracting and provocative, and would be to most players, since it forces you to wonder if a referee isn't needed even for casual matches.

One mode of psychological warfare is to upset an opponent by remarks. For example, a player might say "I see Randy beat you last week 6–0, 6–1. Gee, I don't understand why you had trouble with him. I beat him yesterday 6–2, 6–1." Another—no doubt too silly to be resorted to very often—involves antics and clowning. Frank Kovacs, who was known as the "Clown Prince of Tennis," had a game much like Ilie Nastase's. I often teamed up with Kovacs when we were both in the Army. We won the Allied Tennis Tournament in Brisbane, Australia, many years ago. He was full of antics. In serving he would hold four or five balls in his left hand, toss all of them up, but hit only one. Bobby Riggs, after playing Kovacs, accused him of stalling on changeovers and staging sit-down strikes on the court in protest

82

The author (left) with Frank Kovacs who was known as the "Clown Prince of Tennis" and who was a Finalist in Singles at the 1940 U.S. Open Champions at Forest Hills. They often teamed up together while in the Army and once won the Allied Tennis Tournament in Brisbane, Australia, during World War II.

over line calls. Another time, Riggs came in shorts to play Frankie, who wore long white flannels, which were then in style. Frankie laughed as he pointed to Bobby's shorts. Then Frankie cut his flannels off at the knees, proclaiming, "You don't have a thing on me."

Sometimes the press, wittingly or unwittingly, can be an instrument of psychological warfare in major tournaments. During the 1960 Davis Cup finals at Sidney, Australia, in which the Australian team defeated first the Americans and then the Italians, local papers tore into the American team. Our players were described as tempestuous and impulsive. Any display of emotion on the court was, in the next edition, represented as a temper tantrum or an instance of bad sportsmanship on the part of the American players, who became edgy and, it seemed, distracted. Any player or team covered by the media had best steel his, or its, nerves and feelings to withstand whatever may be said or written. This can be done by facing squarely the fact that completely objective, knowledgeable reporting is never possible, and unbiassed, fair reporting only occasionally so. To accept such failings as part of the way things are is to save oneself from impotent rage and unnerving anxiety.

Psychological warfare through what is said or written need not be limited to abuse or other kinds of harsh verbal assaults. Praise, for instance, can be a way to motivate a player far beyond his usual ability. Ted Schroeder, commenting on the 1958 Davis Cup competition, which the United States team won, revealed that Perry Jones, the team captain, Jack Kramer, and Pancho Gonzales did a snow job on Alex Olmedo by heaping praise on him until he was convinced that he was a truly great player. Olmedo, euphoric and elated from all the verbal bouquets he had been receiving, defeated Australia almost single-handedly. This is in sharp contrast to the incident cited earlier when Pancho Gonzales praised the Italians and downgraded the Australians to the extent that the Italians were lulled into complacency and lost.

Pancho Gonzales was a master at psychological warfare. In his battle with Lew Hoad for the World's Professional Tennis Championship in 1958, Hoad was turning the tour into a complete rout. He won eighteen of the first twenty-seven matches. Gonzales, then owner of the world's fastest and hardest service, applied the skids to Hoad's game in a hurry, however, and evened the tour won-lost record at twenty-one games each. He then went on to win the pro crown. Gonzales' sudden uprising was attributed to two major factors: he had begun playing much better tennis and he had won the psychological war with Hoad by constantly needling him. Gonzales has long been known as the type of player who would try to win any way he could. A steady attempt to break the opposition's concentration is one of his methods. In his battles with Hoad, the steadiness of his efforts was crucial. At first, Hoad was able to withstand Gonzales' needling. It was only after Gonzales had kept up the needling for a good while that Hoad broke and became vulnerable.

If a player wishes to engage in the sort of psychological warfare that enhances his image as a formidable player and undermines his opponent's confidence and playing ability, the general strategy is to induce the opponent to think and act in such a way that he works against himself—becomes his own enemy, so to speak. More specifically, you must get at and call and marshal all the facts and truths that will inspire others to see you in the best possible light and your opponent in the worst. To utter something that everyone knows is false, or merely boastful, will destroy the impression or effect you are trying to create. Your appeals to emotion and your attempts to control attitudes

Jack Kramer was in the Top Ten of the National Ranking five times. He was the U.S. singles champion in 1946 and 1947 and in 1947 won the Wimbledon crown. He was a tough competitor and an aggressive net-rusher who relentlessly played the serve and volley attack. His Big Game success created nations of serve and volley specialists.

Lew Hoad started playing tennis at the early age of eight. The Australian could not get enthusiastic about small tournaments, but in the bigger ones he showed determination and the fight of a tiger. He hit the ball with tremendous power hence earning the nicknames "the bull," "the whip" and "the blacksmith."

must be grounded in fact and good sense—at least they must appear to be. Also, you should avoid antagonizing anyone. Therefore, avoid bragging about your victories; do not deride your opponent's losses; do not resort to insult, ridicule, or mockery. You want the people who will be in contact with your opponent to be either sympathetic to you or, if they are on his side, respectful of you.

For instance, just before the 1969 Davis Cup finals, an Associated Press newsman commented, "The indomitable Arthur Ashe, Jr., and his United States teammates are prohibitive 10–1 favorites to whip the depleted Australian forces and win back the Davis Cup." Australia's cagy captain, Harry Hopman, responded by saying, "This is my greatest challenge. I regard Ashe as the greatest player in the world, amateur or pro, but he *can* be beaten, on a certain day, under certain circumstances." Hopman's first sentence reveals him to be frank, honest, and, implicitly, humble—he makes himself appealing to his audience. His opinion that Ashe is the greatest player in the world is warranted by the facts; Ashe was, indeed, a very great player then—Hopman is credible. And so, when frank, honest, humble, credible Harry Hopman delivers the gaseous generality that "on a certain day, under certain circumstances" Arthur Ashe can be beaten, his utterance has a force and potency to it far in excess of its substance. Moreover, the very emptiness of the generality invites his listeners—among whom was Ashe—to fill up the hollowness with substance; in other words, to look at Ashe and see in him imperfections and weaknesses that could "on a certain day, under certain circumstances" prove to be fatal. As it turned out, Bill Bowrey, the Australian national champion, upset Ashe 2–6, 6–3, 11–9, 8–6.

Now, it's unlikely that Hopman's response to the remark of the AP reporter was a significant factor in Ashe's loss. But then, psychological warfare and gamesmanship should not, and probably cannot, be primary determinants of a tennis match, and it is certainly not the purpose of this chapter to suggest that a player should devote himself or herself to scheming and trickery, as if they were on a par with good strokes and a good attitude. It will suffice if you are simply alert to the kind of thing that does occur, are prepared to handle it when you are the object, and, when circumstances require you to do something extra for your game, know how to dish a little of it out.

One of my tennis partners likes to employ a tactic that might be termed sabotage-by-nonchalance. Bill will step onto the court and just before play begins say something like this: "Walt, I had a T-bone steak a while ago that was out of this world"—Bill is rubbing and patting his belly and putting on a face like that of a Turkish pasha ready for a post-orgy snooze—"and I don't know if I'm going to be able to wield this thing [his racket] for very long.... Maybe we should go for a drive along the shore and look at the sailboats." Since I have worked up my fighting spirit and am ready to go for the kill in our match, this is not the sort of thing I want to hear—and Bill knows it, and that's why he says such things. He is shrewd enough to sense that easy, pleasant remarks about delicious dinners and lovely seashore sights, delivered with suitably lethargic gestures, yawns, and the like, can take the edge off a killer's instincts.

A similar ploy was used by Jean Borotra, an excellent player of the past, who was known as the "Bounding Basque." He was, in his nontennis career, a salesman, and he applied his knowledge of practical psychology to his sport. When he ran into problems on the court, he would sometimes stagger to the net, display all the symptoms of exhaustion or imminent collapse, look with awe at the titan on the other side of the net, and then, having deflated his opponent's resolution and vigilance, proceed to reverse the momentum of the contest and snatch victory from defeat. Bill Tilden once said that after beholding Borotra's "pooped-out" routine you had to make sure that it wasn't you who were near to collapsing. The clever thing about such an act is that the actor, knowing what he is up to, is safe from the effects he creates, whereas the innocent or unsuspecting opponent who takes it all in may, through natural empathy, assume the condition projected by the actor.

But undoubtedly the kind of psychological warfare and gamesmanship that a developing player should be most dedicated to mastering is the kind that he employs against his or her own deficiencies as a player. The work of Ivan Pavlov, the Russian physiologist generally associated with the notion of the "conditioned reflex," and that of B. F. Skinner, the American behavioral psychologist famous for his work in the area of behavior modification, constituted the groundwork for much of what has been utilized by psychologists and others to devise ways whereby people can overcome deficiencies and failings of one kind or another—or, more generally, change the way they behave, act, and/or perform.

Pavlov, you may recall, conditioned dogs to associate the sound of a bell with food, so that eventually he could make his dogs drool by tinkling his bell. Skinner, also employing sounds, conditioned rats to press down on a bar in order to get at food. From such work, operant-conditioning procedures—the use of rewards and punishments to change behavior—have derived. Such procedures have been used not only for purposes of therapy but also to increase the effectiveness of various kinds of instruction and training.

People have different feelings about the desirability of applying such procedures to human beings, and it is not my intention to suggest that tennis players in training play Pavlov or Skinner and use methods resembling theirs on themselves. But I do want to suggest that intelligent, purposeful conditioning employing things akin to rewards and punishments can be used to get more out of practice and training. The insights and discoveries of behavioral psychology, and the practical applications of them, deserve a place in this book because, as we have been seeing all along here, effective playing is the expression of all that makes up a player—technical mastery, physical condition, intelligence and knowledge, frame of mind, state of feeling, and psychological-behavioral makeup.

An account of some operant-conditioning procedures I have used to improve my serve will, I hope, illustrate the matter I have been touching on and encourage developing players, and coaches, to work out comparable procedures of their own for whatever aspects of tennis play they want to work on.

About a year ago I applied a behavior-modification approach to improve my serve. Since I have been playing for decades, it was not realistic to think that I could improve the speed of my serve a great deal, but I felt that if I could improve my placement, I could improve the effectiveness of my serve. Your ability to place the serve is the single best test of your playing ability if you are a tennis player of, say, varsity caliber. The speed of the service as implied by the distance the ball travels from the first to the second bounce is the best way to evaluate a beginner's playing ability. I have learned that accuracy of serve is not improved when speed is decreased.

I set up two target areas in each of the four service courts, as shown in Diagram A. Each target area was two feet wide and eight feet long. I decided that I would practice 100 serves for a period of three months as often as my work schedule permitted. Ideally, this would have been twice a day. Actually, there were times when I was able to practice only once every three days. Most of the time, however, I practiced daily.

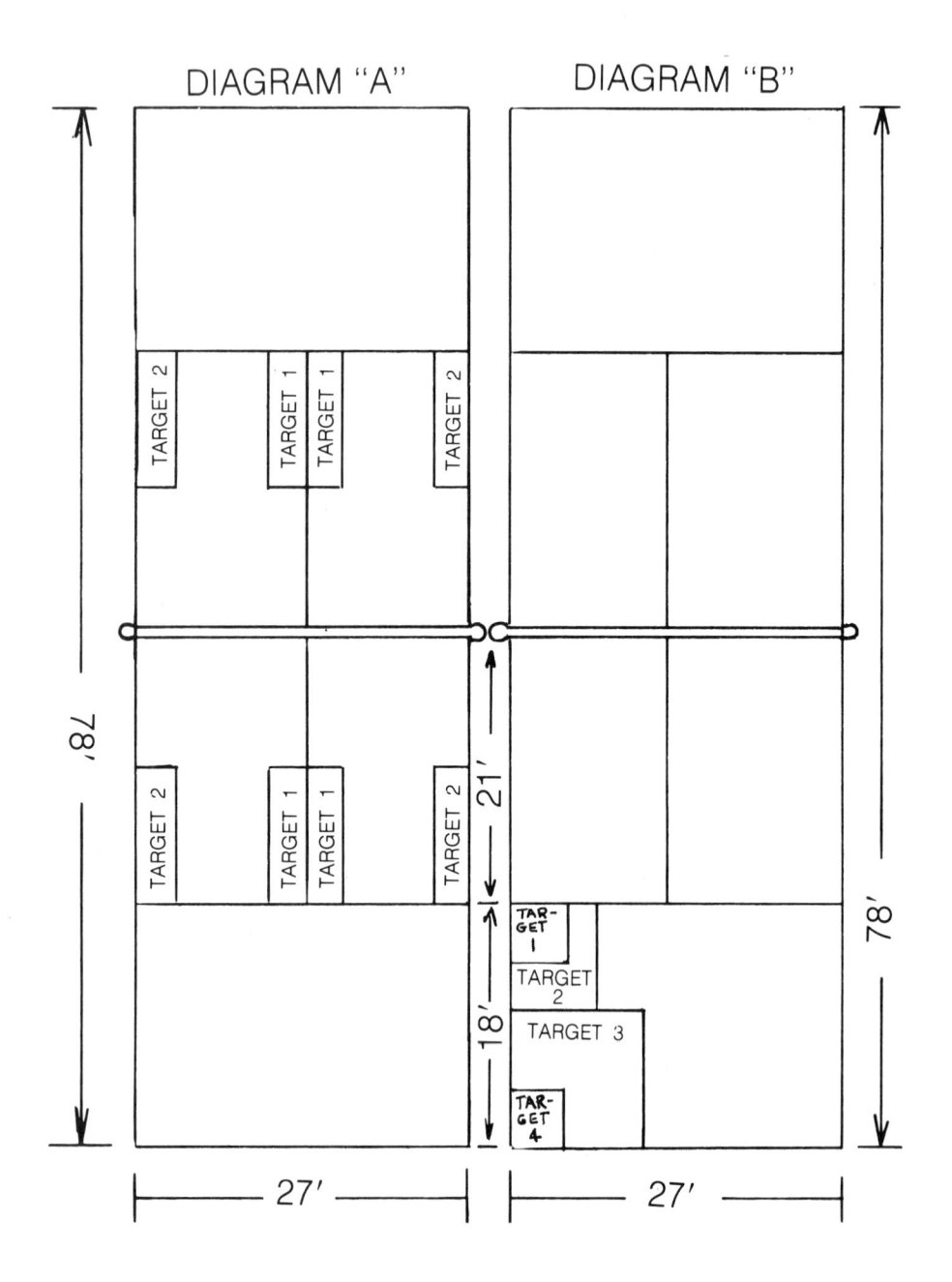

Before starting "target practice," I warmed up by serving about twenty-five balls without much concern for placement. I began serving in the deuce court. My procedure was to start with Target One, and when I hit it to advance to Target Two. When I hit Target Two, I went back to the first, and repeated the procedure until I used all twenty-five balls. I noted the number of "hits" in each of the two targets. Then I repeated the same procedure in each of the other three service courts until I had served 100 times. After each of the twenty-five-ball target-practice sets I wrote down the number of my hits in each of the service courts, using this scorecard:

Date	Service Court		Total hits
	A		
	Target 1	Target 2	
	B		
	Target 1	Target 2	
	C		
	Target 1	Target 2	
	D		
	Target 1	Target 2	
	Total Hits		

I also kept scorecards for the total number of hits on the target for each practice period and the total number of hits on each of the eight targets. These records provided a basis for a reward system. The first five practice sessions were used as a base line. At this time I hit the target thirty times out of a hundred tries. In subsequent periods any score better than this was "rewarded" and a worse score was "punished": I kept a record card in my tennis bag and put the chart on the wall in my den. Hence my progress was clearly visible, and it was in a position where I could point it out to friends, thus gaining for myself approval—a form of reward. I also worked out a system of more tangible rewards. Whenever I scored five hits above the base line of thirty, I would reward myself with my favorite drink after practice. The first time I surpassed the base line by ten points, my wife took me out for a steak dinner. The last five periods of the first month I used to compute a new base line to intensify my competition with myself. My base line went up to forty. Unless a base line is raised periodically it becomes too easy to exceed and the rewards are meaningless. At the end of the first month I was averaging forty-five out of a hundred, an increase of 15 percent in three months.

This improvement was particularly gratifying when one considers that I

Peaches Bartkowicz, ranked several times in the "First Ten," was one of the first women to develop a lethal two-fisted backhand. The "Pigtailed Polish Wonder" from Hamtramck, Michigan, a protégée of the late Jean Hoxie, developed her game through determination, spending hours hitting thousands of tennis balls against the wall. She showed excellent concentration and tremendous confidence in her own ability.

was fifty-five years old at this time. The greatest satisfaction I got came from the comments of my competitors, who wanted to know what I had been doing and what happened that I was playing so much better. Their comments, of course, were another form of reward. Acing one of my competitors seven times in two sets was also a nice reward. I don't remember ever having aced him before in five years of play.

A further bonus from this system was the information gained from the charts that I was twice as good in hitting Target Two as Target One. Dur-

Virginia Wade has the best serve in women's tennis, but has sometimes had trouble keeping her moody and competitive nature under control on the court. She is known for the power and intensity of her will to win at Wimbledon in 1977, when she ultimately beat Chris Evert in three sets. The No. 1 British Champion has a disciplined mind and solid concentration. Known for her determination and killer instinct, she sees the tennis court as a field of mortal combat.

ing a practice session, I analyzed why this was so and found that most of my misses were going to the right of the service line in the add court. This led to the discovery that my stance had to be changed. I experimented with a slightly revised stance and was able to decrease significantly hitting the ball outside the service line in Target One in the add court.

Other aspects of your tennis game can be improved through the same general procedure. For example, if you have access to an adjustable trajectory machine, or have a friend who is willing to work with you and hit balls to your backhand, you can work on returning backhand shots to designated targets on the court.

Behavior-modification principles, especially some of the ones used in therapy for stuttering, can with modifications be applied to tennis coaching. One such procedure involves a series of graduated verbal tasks ranging from the simplest—for example, saying one-syllable words—to difficult ones, such as articulating long, complex sentences. A series of rewards both verbal (praise) and tangible (gifts, and the like) is incorporated in the procedure. No rebukes or other forms of punishment are used. A stutterer is, for instance, shown a number of simple words on flash cards and asked to read each. To each response the therapist will say "Good," "Very good," or "Excellent," depending how free of stuttering the expression is. When the stutterer does extremely well, on occasions the therapist will give him, say, a chocolate soda. Over a period of time stuttering can be substantially reduced by such a method.

A similar procedure might be applied to specific tennis deficiencies; for example, hitting forehand and backhand drives too short. To correct this deficiency the coach would be at the net and hit the ball to the pupil's backhand. The pupil would be aiming for a cross-court target three feet square, two sides of which would be formed by the base line and the sideline, as shown in Diagram B. If the pupil hits the ball in the service area, the coach would say nothing, but if the pupil hits Target One then the coach would say "Good." If he hits Target Two the coach would say "Very good." If he hits Target Three the coach would say "Excellent." If he hits Target Four the coach would reward the pupil with something tangible, like a handshake.

At the end of a training session the coach could give additional positive reinforcement by a prepared encouraging talk. For example, he might say "Ann, you did well today. You worked hard and concentrated. You were eager and determined to improve your backhand down the line, and most of your shots were hit with excellent depth. Nice going!" And, as with my procedure for improving my serve, records and charts should be kept to provide additional motivation and reinforcement.

In the procedure just described, it will be noted that no punishment is used. The nearest thing to punishment is the withholding of praise or reward when the pupil fails to hit the target. Much research has indicated that, in training, praise is more effective than punishment. However, with some individuals and in some circumstances, punishment—perhaps in the form of rebukes—can be effective. So, if the pupil fails to hit a target with his forehand or backhand drives, the coach might call "No" every time the pupil fails. In addition, at the end of the training session the coach can give negative reinforcement by a prepared discouraging talk. He might say "Bill, you did not do well today. You were distracted when the airplane went by; you were not eager to practice your forehand cross-court; and despite my repeated 'No!' you continued to hit your shots short. We'll practice again tomorrow, and let's hope you can do better."

Behavior-modification principles have been used extensively in other areas, and they can obviously be applied to tennis. The suggestions given here have proved their usefulness and will no doubt lead to other innovations in tennis training. Behavior-modification as applied to tennis is not a panacea or even a striking innovation; it is a sensible approach based on our capacity to respond to what is gratifying and to what is not—and therefore on our capacity to change ourselves for the better.

Many players and good coaches have been using behavior-modification methods for years. Not only are such methods effective in learning tennis skills, but they are also a substantial time saver, since, being systematic, they are purposeful and efficient.

Epilogue

Tennis in the United States has come a long way since Miss Mary Ewing Outerbridge, a young society woman of Staten Island, New York, returned from her Bermuda vacation in the winter of 1874. She brought some strange-looking things (rackets, balls, and nets) and set up the first tennis court in America.

Since that time, the world of tennis has been marching on. Today tennis has millions of participants, both players and observers, in the United States and throughout the world. It is a pleasant and entertaining activity for persons of all ages, but at the competitive level it is a game requiring top physical shape, skill, experience, and, above all, mental toughness—determination, concentration, confidence.

Today's champions may become tomorrow's heroes who are no longer in current competition. Later, a few may become legends. Most are forgotten. Richard D. Sears won the first seven U.S. Championships beginning in 1881. Then came the age of Big Bill Tilden and Little John Johnston. This was followed by such champions as Ellsworth Vines, Don Budge, Jack Kramer, Frank Parker, Richard Gonzales, Frank Sedgman, John Newcombe, and Rod Laver.

Many women champions have made their mark on tennis history. These include Suzanne Lenglen, Helen Wills, Helen Jacobs, A. Louise Brough, Maureen Connolly, and Althea Gibson.

More recently the worldwide men champions include such players as Bjorn Borg, John McEnroe, Jimmy Connors, Vites Gerulaitis, Ivan Lendl, Vijay Amritraj, Brian Gottfried, Wojtek Fibak, Eddie Dibbs, Stan Smith, Roscoe Tanner, Harold Solomon, Peter Fleming, and Gene Mayer.

The current worldwide women champions are Martina Navratilova, Chris Evert Lloyd, Tracy Austin, Billie Jean King, Evonne Goolagong Cawley, Wendy Turnbull, Virginia

Wade, Kathy Jordan, Greer Stevens, Sue Barker, Rosemary Casals, Ann Kiyomura, Caroline Stoll, Kathy May Teacher, Kate Latham, and Terry Holladay.

In the meantime other champions have been emerging. In Men's 21 and under the following were the first ten in the 1979 USTA National Rankings: 1. Jay Lapidus 2. Mel Purcell 3. Jim Arias 4. Tony Trear 5. Scott Lipton 6. Jai DiLouie 7. Scott Bondurant 8. Brent Crymes 9. Tim Downey 10. Paul Bernstein.

The first ten women in the 21 and under class were 1. Lucy Gordon 2. Ann Henricksson 3. Susan Gibson 4. Kelly Kruk 5. Kathy Snelson 6. Becky Bell 7. Grace Barrie 8. Catherine Yelverton 9. Jane Natenstadt 10. Heidi Allison.

In Boys' 18 Singles the following were the first ten: 1. Scott Davis 2. Ben Testerman 3. Billy Nealon 4. Rodney Harmon 5. Mike DePalmer 6. Daniel Saltz 7. Randall Nixon 8. Sean Brawley 9. Tom Foster 10. Mark Pinchoff.

The first ten in the Girls' 18 Singles were: 1. May Lou Piatek 2. Andrea Jaeger 3. Alycia Moulton 4. Nina Voydat 5. Kelly Henry 6. Charlene Murphy 7. Anne White 8. Heather Ludloff 9. Susy Jaeger 10. Elise Burgin.

In the Boys' 16 Singles the number one was Sammy Giammalva. He was followed by 2. Matt Anger 3. George Bezecny 4. Mike Pazourek 5. Jonathan Canter 6. Greg Holmes 7. Tim Pawsat 8. Rill Baxter 9. Paul Annacone 10. Michael Kures.

The first ten in the Girls' 16 Singles were 1. Kathy Horvath 2. Kathrin Keil 3. Sue Mascarin 4. Kate Gompert 5. Anrea Leand 6. Zina Garrison 7. Pilar Vasquez 8. Pamela Casale 9. Michelle DePalmer 10. June Ferestien.

In the Boys' 14 Singles Mat Frooman was ranked number one. Behind him were 2. Richy Leach 3. Jonathan Canter 4. Doug Pielet 5. Jimmy Brown 6. Richey Reneberg 7. William Daniel 8. Jeff Chambers 9. Ricky Peck 10. Eric Rosenfeld.

Carol Heynen was ranked one in the Girls' 14 Singles. She was followed by 2. Beverly Bowes 3. Lori Kosten 4. Janet Lagasse 5. Heather Hairston 6. Lisa Bonder 7. Leigh Anne Eldredge 8. Amy Holton 9. Kirstin Laux 10. Meghan McMahon.

The 1979 USTA Boys' 12 Singles rankings included: 1. Jim Williams 2. Robby Weiss 3. Aaron Krickstein 4. John Carras 5. Jon Kass 6. Joseph Blake 7. Jay Berger 8. Chip McColl 9. Todd Kros 10. Jeff Hersh.

The first ten rankings in the Girls' 12 Singles were: 1. Kathy Rinaldi 2. Ginny Purdy 3. Eileen Tell 4. Nicole Stafford 5. Tatjana Schrobsdorff 5. Terry Phelps 7. Michelle Torres 8. Sonia Hahn 9. Debbie Spence 10. Marianne Werdel.

As in the past, some of these current first tenners will be a "flash in the pan" and will not have the physical endurance, skill, experience, and, particularly, mental toughness to persist and come out on top. Others will undoubtedly emerge as tomorrow's champions.

While the players between ages twelve and twenty-one compete for USTA National Rankings and world domination, there is increasing competition among players age thirty-five all the way up to eighty.

The following are the 1979 National "First Ten" in the various divisions:

MEN'S 35 SINGLES. 1. Keith Diepraam 2. Butch Newman 3. Robert Siska 4. Peter Van Lingen 5. Paul Cranis 6. Richard Johnson 7. Larry Nagler 8. Robert McKenna 9. James Parker 10. Len Saputo.

WOMEN'S 35 SINGLES. 1. Susan Starrett 2. Judy Alvarez 3. Cathie Anderson 4. Patricia Cody 5. Sissy Kelly 6. Charleen Hillebrand 7. Marlene Poletti 8. Paule Ferguson 9. Penny

Barrett 10. Ruth Barnett.

WOMEN'S 40 SINGLES. 1. Paule Ferguson 2. Carol Bentley 3. Carol Wood 4. Nancy Reed 5. Eleanor Wright 6. Donna Balchios 7. Martha Post 8. Diana Gai 9. Lee Burling 10. Justine Butler.

MEN'S 45 SINGLES. 1. Russell Seymour 2. King Van Nostrand 3. Cliff Mayne 4. Allen Morris 5. Bob Perry 6. Ron Livingston 7. Jason Morton 8. Heinz Hamza 9. Larry Huebner 10. Roger Sharr.

WOMEN'S 45 SINGLES. 1. Nancy Reed 2. Jane Crofford 3. Olga Palafox 4. Helen Perez 5. Nancy Neeld 6. Betsy Roberti 7. Lorraine Sharp 8. Rosemary Rea 9. Justine Butler 10. Betty Claus.

MEN'S 50 SINGLES. 1. Jason Morton 2. Hugh Stewart 3. Gus Palafox 4. Tom Bartlett 5. Don Gale 6. Ed Kauder 7. Jack Shoemaker 8. Clint Arbuckle 9. Robin Willner 10. Bill Davis.

WOMEN'S 50 SINGLES. 1. Betty Pratt 2. June Gay 3. Kathy Rothfels 4. Vilma Gordon 5. Yoko Taylor 6. Phillis Adler 7. Elizabeth Harper 8. Grace Findlay 9. Frances Wakefield 10. Lovie Beard.

MEN'S 55 SINGLES. 1. Robert Sherman 2. Buck Archer 3. William Parsons 4. Robert Perez and Charles Anderson 6. Harris Everett 7. Jack Laffey 8. David Martin 9. Roger Downs 10. Robert Cage.

WOMEN'S 55 SINGLES. 1. Dodo Cheney 2. Phyllis Adler 3. Lovie Beard 4. Doris Popple 5. Grace Findlay 6. Amy Yee 7. Nancy Penson 8. Beth Oliver 9. Eleanor Harbula 10. Jackie Michel.

MEN'S 60 SINGLES. 1. Bobby Riggs 2. Jack Jossi 3. Harris Everett 4. Charles Lass 5. William Parsons 6. Alex Swetka 7. Robert Galloway 8. George Peebles 9. John McGrath 10. Mickey Pardew.

WOMEN'S 60 SINGLES. 1. Dodo Cheney 2. Jean Corvino 3. Gertrude Amling 4. Pat Yeomans 5. Margo Mahony 6. Jean Selvig 7. Mary Johnston 8. Thelma Merker 9. Ann Hoffman 10. Chris Covington.

MEN'S 65 SINGLES. 1. Gardnar Mulloy 2. Chauncey Steele 3. William Smith 4. Harry Hoffman 5. Charles Swanson 6. William Lurie 7. Jack Staton 8. George Reynolds 9. Walter Cavanaugh 10. John Faunce.

WOMEN'S 65 SINGLES. 1. Margo Mahony 2. Ann Hoffman 3. Peggy Breyak 4. Ruby Bixler 5. Louise Andrews 6. Evelyn Davis 7. Cindy Shands 8. Jacqueline Piatigorsky 9. Rosamond Hyde 10. Berenice Rielley.

MEN'S 70 SINGLES. 1. Frank M. Goeltz 2. Erling Jensen 3. Francis Manis 4. Emil Johnson 5. Fred Meinert 6. Al Miller 7. Wilfred Jones 8. Leonard Dworkin 9. Edward Stafford 10. William Lufler.

MEN'S 75 SINGLES. 1. Clarence Chaffee 2. Mal Clarke 3. Kenneth Beer 4. Wyn Morris 5. Herschel Hyde 6. Theodore Wellman 7. Steve Harris 8. Ralphe Larson 9. Reuel Ritz 10. Mike Bricksin.

MEN'S 80 SINGLES. 1. Abbey Leitch 2. Walter Wesbrook 3. Kirk Reid 4. DeWitt Redgrave 5. Stephen Graves 6. William Mallery 7. Carl Busch 8. T. Jefferson Glover 9. Henry Doyle 10. Jake Pettus.

I cannot say what the tennis champions of tomorrow will be like in terms of physical shape, skills, and experience. But I am confident that the mental toughness of these tennis champions will continue to improve, and this will be made possible by continual understanding and application of determination, concentration, and confidence.

ABOUT THE AUTHOR

Dr. Walter A. Luszki is a clinical and educational psychologist in private practice, Charleston, South Carolina. He has combined two interesting fields in *Winning Tennis through Mental Toughness*—his profession as a psychologist and his major leisure-time activity as a tennis player. He does not claim to be a great tennis champion, but his knowledge of psychology has helped him improve his game and his enjoyment of the sport.

Dr. Luszki has played tennis for more than 50 years. He won his first championship in Detroit when he was 13. Since then, he has won some 250 tennis trophies, including the State of South Carolina Closed Men's 60 Singles Champion in October, 1977, and the 1977 Men's 45 and 55 Singles in Charleston. He was ranked 29th in the nation in Men's 60 Singles in 1976. This ranking was largely based on his reaching the finals in the National Clay Court Championships in the Little Rock, Arkansas Men's 60 Singles. In addition, he has won academic, college, military, municipal, and state titles from Australia to Europe.

The Army offered many opportunities to play internationally ranked tennis players. As a captain during WW II, Dr. Luszki was chosen as Frank Kovacs's doubles partner in tournament play. They won the allied Tennis Tournament in Brisbane, Australia, in 1943.

Dr. Luszki's professional credentials are equally impressive. He is a graduate of the University of Michigan in psychology, and received his doctorate from the University of Georgia in 1964, following retirement from the United States Army. Dr. Luszki has taught and lectured extensively, and has contributed many articles to professional journals. He has been published in magazines such as *World Tennis, Tennis U.S.A., Tennis Illustrated,* and *Tennis Trade*.

Before retiring to enter private practice, Dr. Luszki had been chief psychologist for the Vince Moseley Evaluation and Diagnostic Clinic in Charleston for several years.